5 FEB 1997

C000128740

THE MUSIC BUSINESS

ANDREW BLAKE

Series Editor: John Izod, Department of Film and
Media Studies, University of Stirling

B. T. Batsford Ltd, London

© Andrew Blake 1992
First published 1992

Typeset by Servis Filmsetting Ltd, Manchester
and printed in Great Britain by BPCC Hazells Ltd

for the publishers
B.T. Batsford Ltd
4 Fitzhardinge Street
London W1H 0AH

A CIP catalogue record for this book
is available from the British Library

ISBN 0 7134 6659 6

To Simon, Ingrid and Molly

CONTENTS

PREFACE

This book is about music, but not a particular category of music. It tries to write about all forms of music, popular, classical, jazz, world music and so on, as subject to the constraints of 'the music business'. It would have been very difficult to write such a piece 20 years ago. We owe the questioning of categories of quality and taste to the rise of cultural studies as an academic subject, and writing about music in particular to a few authors who explored their enthusiasm for popular music through the disciplines of sociology. Thanks in particular to the work of Simon Frith, popular music is now an expanding and confident field of study; most work on music written within the cultural studies framework owes a lot, if as in this case indirectly, to his example.

Many students at the Polytechnic of East London have been helpful and enthusiastic contributors to my attempts to understand the business of music, and I am most grateful to them and to all my colleagues in the Department of Cultural Studies. The level of mutual interest and help there is astonishing given the current siege mentality of so many academic departments, and it is a great pleasure to work in such a supportive environment. I should also pay tribute to the many musicians whose music, musicianship and enthusiasm has kept my own interest on the boil; in particular to my former colleagues in Man Jumping, especially Glyn Perrin; and to Gillian Moore, Lucy Wilson, Elise Lorraine, Patricia Guigui, Alan Durant, and the dedicatees of this book. The expansion of music technology has been another source of continued interest (and occasional frustration). My friends at *Music Technology* magazine have provided many opportunities for discussion of the joys and sorrows of microchip-based music-making. Tim Goodyer's contribution to the final product will be obvious – and I'm very grateful. Writing this book was made a more congenial task through the hospitality of Denise, Mike, Rowena and Hazel, and was often pleasantly interrupted by the feline priorities of Matilda and Edwin. The book was wordprocessed on an Amstrad PPC640 and an Elonex 286M, using Wordperfect, which worked well. Finally I should pay tribute to the series editor, John Izod, and especially to the patience of Anthony Seward at Batsford.

Acknowledgments

All photographs are ©Tim Goodyer except where indicated. I am grateful to Tim, to Lesley Crewdson, and to the Trustees of the Victoria and Albert Museum, for permission to use photographs. The author and publishers have made every effort to obtain copyright permission for all the images used in this book. Any enquiries about copyright material should be made to the publisher in the first instance.

Introduction

This book is about music and the making of music. It aims to answer a single question: what do we mean by 'music' in the 1990s? The question is simple enough, but there is no straightforward answer. There are several immediate problems we have to solve in order to answer it: who is involved in the making of music, and why; and who listens to music, and why. We will also have to ask what we mean by terms like 'popular music', 'jazz', 'world music' and 'classical music'.

We take these boundaries almost for granted. But how solid are they? Can we even identify strong boundaries between 'popular music' and 'classical music'? A few reflections on my experience of the London music scene in the summer of 1990 will begin to illuminate the complexity of the question. Most people would agree that the pop charts are a reasonable place to start if we want to define 'popular music'. A single release of 'Nessun dorma', an aria from an opera by Puccini sung by Italian tenor Luciano Pavarotti, reached number 2, and stayed in the charts for two months. At the same time two albums by violinist Nigel Kennedy, featuring music by 'classical' composers Vivaldi and Mendelssohn, entered the top 10 in the pop album charts. Kennedy has also made albums of jazz and jazz-rock fusion. At rock venue the Hammersmith Odeon the English Chamber Orchestra played a concert of eighteenth-century classical music by Vivaldi and Mozart using the light show and amplification of the rock concert, and promising 'classical music – very loud' in their advance publicity. A few days later at classical music venue the Royal Festival Hall the Kronos String Quartet ended their recital of contemporary classical music by playing arrangements of music by r'n'b star Bo Diddley and rock guitarist Jimi Hendrix. A Caribbean steel band played at London's premier symphony concert series, the Proms. At another classical venue, the Barbican Centre, I saw a concert by John Harle, a saxophonist who has been called the outstanding classical saxophonist of today. He wasn't playing classical pieces, but jazz-rock fusion, with a band playing high technology electronic instruments. This band shared a bill with half a dozen other sax players, young turks and middle-aged session players, playing more conventional jazz accompanied by a more traditional trio of string bass, piano and drums. All these concerts were very well attended (and without any obvious signs of public protest at such a breaking down of barriers).

Of course you could also go to more conventional gigs, in the summer of 1990. You could see classical concerts with unamplified orchestras playing symphonies; rock gigs in all shapes and sizes, from Madonna in front of 70,000 at Wembley to pub bands entertaining a hundred or so, playing anything from Beatles songs, through 1960s soul to electronic dance music. You could go to jazz gigs in seedy clubs attended by the faithful few; and you could see and hear many musics from all over the world: Irish, Turkish, Greek, Indian, African and so on, playing for enthusiastic and cosmopolitan audiences. Meanwhile on the radio you could hear black music of various kinds, jazz, hip-hop and reggae; album rock; and much more ethnic music, all on pirate radio stations; there was 24-hour black and dance music and 24-hour jazz on new legitimate radio stations for the first time; alongside old and new pop, easy listening, and classical musics on established public and commercial radio stations. Land-based television offered fragments of a similar mixture, while on satellite television you could see operas and non-stop pop videos. There may be no easy way to define popular music, but music of all sorts is very popular. All these gigs and forms of broadcasting are available because significant numbers of people want to perform, or write, music, and because most people attend gigs or listen at home to an enormous variety of musical forms.

Music is clearly a powerful and important part of most people's lives. It surrounds us, whether we like it or not: on television and the radio, in airport lounges and bars, in sports stadia and supermarkets, music is a continuous feature of the background. But most of us also make a special effort to use music in some way: by playing or singing, by composing, and most often by listening at concerts or at home. This book aims to explore the power of music by adding one further deceptively simple question to 'What do we mean by music?': 'Just who is responsible for the music which surrounds us?' A commonsense answer might be that it is the *artists*, the star singers and musicians. They make the recordings which we as consumers buy, they are featured on the promotional videos we see on TV, and they often tour to promote their recordings, and so provide us with live gigs to go to. However, artists hardly ever make records by themselves: they may receive help from songwriters and arrangers, session musicians and backing groups, record producers and recording engineers. Albums, cassettes and CDs are recorded in studios and mass produced in factories, and the money to record almost always comes from record companies. The music business is just that: a business, a highly profitable part of consumer capitalism.

This obvious point often leads people to think of the music business as a conspiracy, which offers us the constant repetition of successful, bland formulas, and manipulates us emotionally and politically, as well as economically. Conspiracy theories are not new. Critics of formula pop music produced by high technology instruments such as samplers were anticipated by George Orwell, who warned about the use of music manufactured by machines in his book *1984*. It is hard to identify any actual conspiracy, but there is some truth in this view. Many top 40 hits are made according to a successful formula, by producers who program computers but remain behind the scenes, without much intervention by the named

Stock, Aitken and Waterman, plus synthesizer and mixing desk: the successful late 1980s combination that postponed the 'death of the single'.

artists, who may not even play or sing on 'their' records. Many don't play or sing in public appearances either, but merely mouth words to a pre-recorded backing tape while they dance in front of a camera – like duo Milli Vanilli, who lost their Grammy award in December 1990 when they admitted that they were only pretty faces. In cases like this, who is responsible? Obvious candidates would be the *songwriter*, the *record producer* and the *recording engineer*. Many people combine two or more of these roles, and certainly in the case of the British songwriting team Stock, Aitken and Waterman, they have achieved a great deal of success by repeating formulas without very much help from the 'artists' whose names appear on the records. This is not a new phenomenon. American producer Phil Spector was behaving in exactly the same way (and also with great success) in the early 1960s.

However, this conspiracy theory doesn't apply to all music; not even to all chart music. Most artists work in more balanced ways with their producers and sound engineers: Michael Jackson and Quincy Jones, for instance, had an established and creative partnership which produced three successful albums. Others choose to work together on a single-album basis, again often with fruitful results – as for example producer Nile Rogers with David Bowie on the very influential *Let's Dance* album in 1984. Again, some artists like Prince, and British singer-songwriter Kate Bush, remain in complete control of their recordings, writing songs, producing and mixing them, as well as playing and singing.

Artistic control, however complete, doesn't guarantee either creative or financial success. Kate Bush has never been really successful in the USA, despite the best efforts of her record company. And the record company really does have the last word. Prince is a megastar, no doubt loved as passionately by his record company as by his fans. He makes WEA a fortune, and they usually release whatever he tells them to, which has included a great deal of uninteresting formula material as well as the many moments of inspiration. But in December 1987 WEA refused to release a finished Prince album, known as the Black Album. Hundreds of thousands of copies which had been pressed were pulped. The few thousand already in circulation instantly became very valuable collectors' items. Apparently the lyrics were obscene even by Prince's standards. Clearly in this example at least the industry was using its power and exercising censorship. Radio and television companies also occasionally censor records, although when they do the resulting publicity usually guarantees success for the record involved – the Sex Pistols in 1976, and Frankie Goes to Hollywood in 1984, had huge hits partly because radio stations refused to play their records. In the end, though, we can't simply credit artists or producers, or even the owners of record companies or radio or television stations, for the music which surrounds us. We also have to credit (or blame) ourselves as users. The music business remains highly profitable because we buy music

Whose control? He looks just like a puppet pop star, but **Gary Numan was always in control of his own image**, as well as his own records. So much so, in fact, that the music business, which prefers puppets, didn't build on his early success.

software – videos, CDs, singles, cassettes and albums. We consume these products. But we don't consume them in a vacuum. Most obviously, we play the products through other consumer products – *hardware* items such as the video recorder, television, hi-fi, ghetto blaster, walkman and so on. But just as importantly, we consume our chosen music in the context of our own lives and lifestyles: as schoolchildren, young adults, housewives or pensioners, we use the music offered by the industry in different ways to accompany the daily and weekly rituals of work and play. We choose music, styles and moods of music, to accompany the clothes we wear, the cars we drive, and the places we choose to live in and relax.

This may seem to answer the question. It doesn't. There is no simple equation whereby consumer demand is taken note of by the music industry, and then happily supplied; or demand artificially created by a manipulative industry to which consumers happily respond. The consumer and the music business are not completely happy with each other. Although in many ways the range of musical styles on offer has increased, there is a perceptible conservatism in the recording industry which is reflected in the products on offer and the way they are marketed. The industry's continuing concerns over copyright, while they protect the industry's profitability, are also conservative, in that they often interfere with consumer choice. The industry has consistently tried to stop theft of copyright through illegal recording. There was for several years an effective embargo on the sale of the DAT digital tape recording system as a home recording medium in Europe and the USA (though it has been widely available in Japan since 1986, and will probably be more widely available to domestic consumers by the time you read this). Meanwhile the record industry still continues its campaigns – begun in the early 1970s with the slogan 'home taping is killing music' – against the consumer's right to the full use of the familiar analogue compact cassette, and in many countries the price of blank tapes includes a levy paid to record companies. Throughout Europe, the price of compact discs has remained very high, unjustifiably high given the very low unit costs of the medium: after a series of complaints in the British press, a consumer boycott was attempted in the UK in August 1990, but with no immediate success.

Music is indeed powerful and important. Power is in fact a key word in the understanding of the ways in which music works. There is a kind of 'power circuit' which supports the production and consumption of music. Like an electric circuit, all the parts of the circuit have to be completed for the thing to work at all, but some parts of the circuit are more important than others. The next chapter will elaborate on this model: it will provide a theoretical background which we can draw on as we explore the various constituent parts of the music business and work towards a more complete answer to those questions asked at the beginning: just what is music, and who is responsible for it?

2 The power circuit

The guitar is still the most powerful symbol of popular music-making. As any lead guitarist will tell you, feedback is an important part of music-making with an electric guitar. Hold your guitar close to its loudspeaker, and the note will sustain, indefinitely if you want it to. The sound from the loudspeaker feeds back to the guitar's strings, which carry on vibrating. The same guitarist will describe the feeling of power playing gives. Meanwhile, heavy metal fans will also describe their feelings of identification with the music they hear at gigs – they feel a part of the same musical power. The audience, by enjoying and paying for the gig, actually provides part of the means by which the sound is sustained: players, instruments and audience together form a *power circuit*.

Any kind of power is only sustainable if it is part of a circuit. Without the continual feedback of emotional approval and financial support, any form of music-making will eventually grind to a halt.

Zapp. The guitar's power is over-symbolized by the shaping of the body as rifle. The player uses his teeth to play, thus indicating his debt to one of the great guitar heros, Jimi Hendrix.

In the same way that cars stop working unless their fuel tanks are replenished, so musics can disappear if their conditions of making are not sustained. Power has to be maintained and reinvented, or it disappears.

Power is part of all cultural production, and therefore of all music, however and wherever it is made. Power relationships are expressed in many different ways, but they are present in folk music as much as in heavy metal. The ability to play an instrument or sing well enough to give others pleasure confers on some people the power to earn money as musicians. The ability to pay for music to be made (by buying a single, or a ticket for a gig, or by promoting gigs or providing the money to record music) also gives power. In rock music, the existence of power is obvious: clearly, with most rock music instruments, the common power source of electricity is the very basis of their existence. Instruments and the people who play them *express* power, but they also *use* it. Music needs a direct power source: the power of the human body, in the case of the voice and of older instruments like violins, flutes, and drums. Muscles make music, whether you're scraping a bow across a string, blowing across a hole, or hitting a skin with a stick. In the case of rock music, both human power and electricity are necessary. The most expensive electric guitar will remain silent unless it is plugged into an electric power circuit, and then played by someone: without electricity the modern music business is unimaginable.

This is an important point. Even to begin to make the kinds of music we all take for granted today we need the electric power provided constantly by the power stations of advanced industrial society. Music surrounds us in recorded form, as inescapable 'background music' in supermarkets or airport lounges, or more pleasurably as recordings chosen by listeners on the hi-fi at home. All these forms of listening require amplifiers, loudspeakers and decoding equipment such as radio tuners, record or cassette decks or CD players, which are produced in factories, and which use electricity. Modern industrial society produces the power for all this in the obvious sense, with its generating stations and its network of electric cables, plugs and switches providing the electricity for the making and broadcasting of music. It produces the equipment on which music is made and heard, the musical instruments like guitars and keyboards, the recording equipment like multi-track tape recorders and mixing desks, the broadcasting equipment like radio transmitters, and the receiving equipment like ghetto blasters and hi-fi systems. Just as importantly, industrial society and its cities, suburbs and towns provide both the people who make the music and the audience for it, through the concert venues, the recording studios

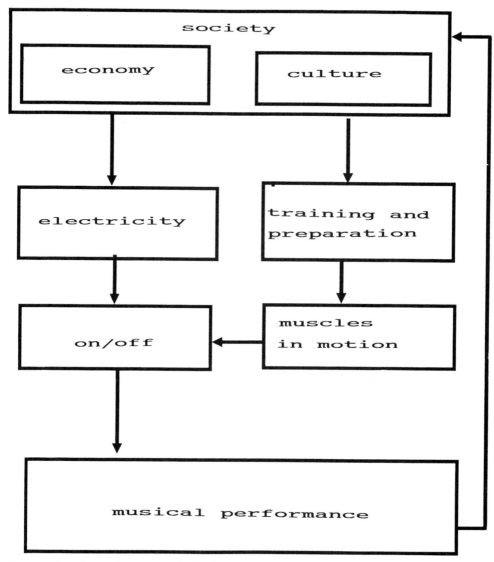

Power and musical performance: a feedback circuit.

and radio and television stations.

None of this 'just happens', naturally. Industrial society is the product of centuries of historical development. It involves the set of economic relationships commonly called capitalism. In this system the private and corporate ownership of money and property structure the ways in which commodities and information are produced and used, and therefore the ways in which we live. Music is both a commodity (in the physical sense of printed sheet music and recordings on CD or cassette) and information (in the sense of sound on the airwaves, decoded from broadcasts or recordings, and experienced at gigs). It is always owned, in both these senses, but not usually simply by one individual or company. Composers and songwriters, musicians and record producers, publishers and record companies, and the people who buy recordings, share the ownership of recorded music in ways which distribute wealth unequally.

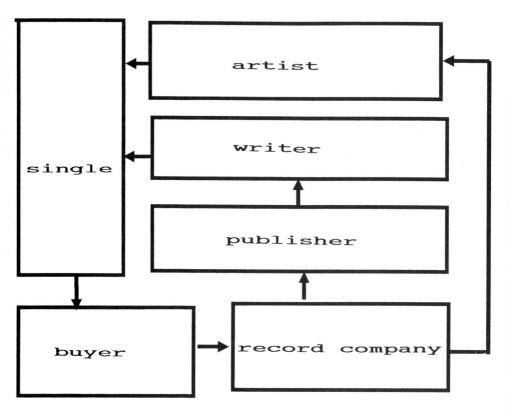

Who actually owns the single? People in any of these categories might claim to.

Power is expressed through this network of economic relationships. But this is not simply a question of ownership, distributed among a set of potentially equal individuals. Inequality is also structured into industrial society, and the power circuits of class, gender and race are also always present in the social, geographic and economic structure of contemporary music making. They are present every time we switch on the hi-fi to play another compact disc, and every time we plug our instruments and amplifiers into the wall sockets to make music. This chapter will examine some of these relationships, and the ways in which they condition music-making today. We begin by looking at the questions of power and music in time and space.

Music and power in time: a brief history

Of course music has a history, but historical writing about music is usually limited in its form and ambition. The most common model for historical writing in the Western world since the eighteenth century has been a story of progress. Historians of European 'classical' music have adopted various versions of this 'progressive' story, and have provided patterns which historians of other musics follow. The story of classical music is often written as a sequence of developments led by influential individuals of successive generations, who build on the previous generation's work to progressively enrich forms such as the symphony. This way of writing about classical music, which traces developments stressing 'progress' through the music of 'great' composers such as Bach (1730s), Mozart (1780s), Beethoven (1820s) and Brahms (1870s) has been copied in some writing about other musics. In *jazz*, for example, the swing of the 1930s (great figure: Duke Ellington) develops into the be-bop of the 1940s (great figure: Charlie Parker) and this in turn develops into the hard bop of the 1950s (great figure: Miles Davis). It is also possible to trace lines of descent in *rock* music through the rock'n'-roll of Elvis in the 1950s, the songwriting of the English beat groups like the Beatles and the Who in the 1960s, the 'progressive music' of the late 1960s (great figures such as Frank Zappa, Yes) to music which is very much aware of all this history, and continually reflects on it, as in the work of Dire Straits or particular albums such as Donald Fagen's *The Nightfly* (1982). The history of *pop*, on the other hand, is very difficult to write in this way; it is more usually one of successive, not progressive, styles and performers. One of the differences between 'pop' and 'rock', always so difficult to define, is that rock music has a sense of historical development, while pop deliberately refuses such a serious approach. In pop there are always stars serving out chunks of disposable music which will be forgotten as soon as they have left the charts. Succeeding generations of pop stars merely do the same things. If you think of history in the European sense of continuous progressive development, then pop lies outside history.

However, these definitions *are* very difficult to sustain. It is, for instance, very difficult to fit black musics like soul, funk and rap into either category – the category 'rock' often seems to exclude black music. Another argument about music in history would be that since the 1980s it is pop music which has been the developing force, using the new technologies and multicultural mixes of style; these arguably make DJ-based bands like Deee-Lite and Massive Attack much more 'progressive' than say U2 or the Stone Roses.

But even the 'progressive' approach constructs a history of music which ignores the rest of history. Social, economic and political changes always *enable* certain ways of making music, and *disable* others. The (rare) historian of music who is aware of these other changes and the ways in which they influence music writes a very different history of music. Far from being an ordered progression with its own internal rules of development, this is a story of power relationships, of struggles between groups contending for power and influence, and the musics they have used to express and reinforce their power. In this version, the history of jazz is not simply of styles like swing and great innovative musicians like Miles Davis, but of the continuing struggle among black Americans to make a music which expresses their own experience, and to have that music recognized and respected by society at large, and of the continuing (positive and negative) responses to the music and the struggle from within white America, and later Europe. The positive responses include the attempt by white musicians from Bix Beiderbecke on to become accepted as jazz musicians by blacks, the warm welcome given to American jazz musicians in Paris, and the jazz-influenced compositions of Gershwin and Stravinsky. The negative responses include stories of discrimination among white-owned record companies, radio stations and concert promoters against jazz and other black musics, and the attempts by the Nazi and Soviet regimes to prevent German and Russian musicians from playing jazz (and their citizens from listening or dancing to it).

In a similar way, the history of pop music's continually changing fashions can be written as continuing tensions between, for example, the desire of young people to make music in their own ways, and the desire of record companies to make reliable profits by selling similar-sounding, safe products. The way in which the music business has become more flexible in responding to (and in some instances trying to lead) changing youth music fashions, puts pop music back into a history of development: the development of the leisure industry, towards today's multi-media integrated marketing developments. This story cannot be written without taking into account the complex power relationship between youth tastes and creativity and capitalism's search for profit.

So there is no single, accepted history of music. There are alternative histories of music, and people should be made aware of them, partly because a unilinear history of music always tends to privilege some forms and developments over others. The music of the powerful in any society is far more likely to survive and to be valued by succeeding generations. We know far more about the 'classical' music of the eighteenth century – the music of composers like Bach,

Handel, Haydn and Mozart – than we do about music made in the villages of eighteenth-century Europe by ordinary people. This is partly because the 'classical' composers served the elite, the wealthy merchants and aristocrats; partly because their music was written down and thus has been preserved in some form (although there remain debates about how to interpret what was written down), whereas much 'folk' music was learned and performed without notation; but most importantly, because the music has been adopted by the continuing elite as 'their' music. Music which has built on the tradition of performance and notation values developed by eighteenth-century composers and their successors has constantly been valued by the elite as 'the best'. Other forms – folk music, and more recently jazz and pop music – were not seen as important by this elite. The popular musical forms have therefore had less social power (people from the elite are unlikely to become performers or writers of popular music, and thus this power circuit is reinforced as popular music remains the province of people outside the elite). Classical music and opera were and are often supported by the state. Popular musics have very seldom attracted state subsidy, and popular musicians and music have seldom attained political power in the ways achieved by, for example, Verdi's operas as a symbol of the movement for national unity in nineteenth-century Italy, or the music of Beethoven, Bruckner and especially Wagner in Nazi Germany.

This situation has changed in recent history, as two important examples show. Firstly, since the Civil Rights movement of the early 1960s in the United States, jazz has been validated as the cultural property of black Americans. Before the 1960s jazz, with its stress on improvisation rather than composition, was often seen as aesthetically inferior to music composed in the Western tradition. The musicians who were seen as successful jazz composers were whites like Paul Whiteman and George Gershwin. The marches and riots of Civil Rights led state policy to be more positive about black American cultural achievements, of which jazz was the most obvious. One prominent change was in education: black music became a common subject of study alongside classical music at the universities and music schools. The new validation, expressing the new-found power of this social group, was symbolized when President Nixon gave a birthday party for jazz composer Duke Ellington at the White House (and earnestly tried to play 'Happy birthday to you' on the piano in front of a rather embarrassed Ellington!).

Secondly, since the 1960s, 'rock' music has come to be seen as the cultural property of Americans who have grown up since the mid-1950s. Rock'n'roll was greeted with suspicion and hostility in the

1950s, both by the musical elite and existing 'Tin Pan Alley' popular songwriters. Again this was partly because of its origins, in rhythm'n'blues and country music. It was said to be music which would only interest blacks, the poor and badly educated, and teenagers, who would soon grow out of it. It would never appeal to the mass of Americans with most money to spend, and would soon be consigned to minority interest. But rock'n'roll refused to die, and indeed it has been part of musical life ever since the 1950s. Like black music, rock music has appeared on the syllabus as a subject of study throughout American education. As importantly, it has remained commercially successful. Many of the generation of teenagers who first listened to rock'n'roll still listen to some form of rock music; and these are people with money to spend. In a capitalist society, this success has been recognized, and rock music has become as politically influential as any other part of big business. Again, presidential blessing has been conferred. Despite continuing hostility to rock music from some influential religious groups, which campaign against obscene or blasphemous lyrics, appreciation of the music has become very important in American politics. No presidential campaign would be complete without candidates professing their admiration for musicians like Bruce Springsteen or Stevie Wonder – and all too often, the 'stars' return that praise and help to raise funds for their important fans' election campaigns. The astonishing sight of President Bush at his inaugural party, taking the stage with rock stars of the 1970s such as Rod Stewart and Joe Cocker, and *pretending to play a guitar*, showed how close rock music is to the ruling elite. It is no longer simply music for teenagers, the poor, or ethnic minorities. It is a success story of contemporary capitalism, and one of the outstanding success stories of post-war American culture.

Rock music has moved through history to this point of social approval and political power. Claims used to be made for the politics of rock in the 1960s and 1970s: it was seen as libertarian and subversive. The 'Woodstock generation' was also the anti-Vietnam war generation, and the sound of guitarist Jimi Hendrix torturing 'The Star-Spangled Banner' is often played as evidence of the anti-establishment attitude of rock music in the late 1960s. In the case of the 'Rock against Racism' campaign in the UK in the late 1970s, musical collaboration between punk, reggae and other bands seems to have played a part in defeating the electoral success of the extreme right-wing National Front. And in the summer of 1990 President Vaclav Havel of Czechoslovakia told Lou Reed, former member of Velvet Underground and successful solo performer, that rock music had been a continuing focus for opponents of the

Rap star joins the Bush inner circle

Martin Walker in Washington

A SELF-PROCLAIMED "Nigger With Attitude" who joined the ranks of the wealthy with obscene and anti-police rap lyrics went to lunch with President Bush yesterday as a paid-up member of the Republican Senatorial Inner Circle.

Clad in a black leather suit, baseball cap and clanking gold jewellery, the rap star, Eazy-E, sat with the 1,400 dark-suited Republican stalwarts, drank mineral water with his lunch, and applauded the President's speech politely.

There was no performance of his hit, Fuck Tha Police, with its chorus: "Without a gun and a badge, what do you got? A sucker in a uniform, waiting to get shot, By me or another nigger and with a gat, It don't matter if he's smaller or bigger."

Eazy-E received a letter of invitation to join the Inner Circle from the extremely conservative Texas senator, Phil Gramm. One of the more creative forms of political fund-raising, the Inner Circle uses up-market credit card membership lists to recruit supporters who are prepared to fork out $1,000 (£558) in annual dues for a lunch with Mr Bush and regular conferences with other Administration officials and party leaders.

Eazy-E, under his real name Eric Wright, got another letter from the Republican Senate leader, Robert Dole, which read: "Elizabeth and I are especially excited about the news of your nomination, because we will have the chance to be with you."

The lead singer of the group NWA, whose initials stand for Niggers With Attitude, sent his $1,000 in membership and another $230 registration fee for the two-day conference in Washington. But he is not a Republican. "I'm neutral. But it's pretty nice coming here. It's cool."

The Guardian newspaper, 20 March 1991, reports a rebel with a new cause: popular music is now a crucial part of the mainstream American political scene.

communist regimes in Eastern Europe, overthrown in 1989.

However, popular music is not 'naturally' on the side of the left or the politically progressive. In the USA at least this is one reason why rock is so politically powerful. Jon Bon Jovi displays the American flag at his gigs with patriotic pride, where 20 years ago Hendrix might have burned it. English and American rock musicians are now themselves part of the elite; in the sense not only that they can go to the same parties as the political and economic leaders of the world, but increasingly that they can and do use their popularity to influence political life. Far from being obviously 'left' or 'right', in fact, some musicians' direct interventions have changed the agenda of world politics. Bob Geldof's campaign against starvation in sub-Saharan Africa, which led to the Band Aid single and the Live Aid worldwide concert, and Sting's continuing and well-publicized concern for the future of the Amazon rain forests, are obvious examples. There are some musicians who continue to attract the label 'political subversive': Nigerian singer Fela Kuti has been imprisoned because he is seen as a political danger to the regime. Many other musicians, however, are very aware of their influential role within existing political systems. We have seen a film star President of the United States (Ronald Reagan), and a classical pianist, Paderewski, as President of Poland. It cannot be too long before a popular musician becomes a political leader. It is unlikely that whoever it is will be less competent than political leaders drawn from other walks of life.

Music in space: a brief musical geography

Music exists in time, and one approach to its study is to look at changing forms and power structures over time. But music also exists in space, which has its own set of power relationships. The power associated with industrial society has changed the allocation of power and musical space both within countries and between them. Ways of funding musical composition and performance, and the techniques of performance also, have changed. To return to the music of the eighteenth-century elite, for example, the concert tradition of classical music and opera developed in growing urban areas, from the middle of the eighteenth century. Before this time formally trained musicians worked for the traditional patrons, the churches, and the courts of the monarchies and aristocracies of Europe (the only people who could afford to pay them). They were the personal servants of aristocrats and bishops, in the same position as butlers or grooms. The growing cities provided large numbers of people who could not *individually* employ musicians, but who could *collectively* subscribe to concerts. So the concert series, and the concert tour of big cities, which are still undertaken by opera singers and rock musicians today, were established to serve this new 'middle class' audience. Composers and orchestras began to work in specific urban areas, as they still do (we have the London Symphony Orchestra and the New York Philharmonic Orchestra in the same way as we have urban football teams – such as Manchester United or the Dallas Cowboys).

Similarly, many people see today's popular music as first and foremost the product of the city. The ethnic and cultural mix of the modern city allows for that interaction of musical traditions which is so important to the sound of today's music. Even where the various ethnic communities keep closely to themselves in 'ghetto' areas, even in the extreme example of the South African apartheid system, cultural interactions are possible. Music from different countries and from rural areas is constantly available to serve these communities – and anyone else who happens to be around. Local radio stations offering Turkish, Greek, Indian, black American and Caribbean musics are freely available in metropolitan centres like London or New York. Social controls are looser than in village or town, allowing young people the space to mix across these cultures, and to organize themselves and their own musical responses to their experiences. Thus rock'n'roll emerged in the southern United States, most obviously in Memphis with Elvis Presley's first recordings on the Sun label, as an interaction between urban black American rhythm'n'blues and rural black and white American country musics. And in the 1980s Prince reversed the process in Minneapolis, drawing on virtually all the traditions of black American soul and white English and American rock to produce a new fusion of musical styles.

Space inside the city is also important. Modern cities are divided along lines of class and available space. In England, the middle class usually chooses to inhabit semi-detached or detached suburban houses with gardens. They live in semi-isolation, therefore, often with very little sense of community, with young people often spending a great deal of time in their bedrooms (which is where a great many bands are started and songs are written). Poorer people with less choice usually have to live in the cramped tenements and tower blocks of the inner cities. There is more mutual knowledge here, and more sense of community, as the street rather than the bedroom or school is likely to be the basis of young people's lives. The clear divide between the inner city and the suburbs often produces clear divisions of musical taste. In England in the late 1950s the many inner-city teenagers devoted to rock'n'roll celebrated this music in a culture of dance, sexual contact and violent group conflict. Many suburban teenagers joined in with this celebration by bussing or driving in to the centres. They were shadowed, however, by a group of (mainly) suburban young men with an obsessive interest in jazz, which for them expressed perfectly the alienation they felt in suburban life. The 'Beats' in America, and their European equivalents, identified in particular with the touring jazz musician. Mythologized as black, a drug addict, and perpetually lonely, he was seen as rejected by society yet transcending this rejection through his art. He was the 'other', the complementary opposite to the bland individualism of the suburban experience.

In England in the late 1960s the 'hippy' movement was largely middle class and suburban. It copied the movement started in the Haight Ashbury suburb of Los Angeles, and was in many ways based on several related musical styles often lumped together under the catch-all titles 'progressive' or 'underground music'. Hippy tendencies included drug use, pacifism, and some very halting steps towards questioning the place of women in society (the conflict around sexuality and gender roles in this movement was one of the forces behind the Women's Liberation movement in America). Rivalling the hippies in late 1960s Britain was the 'skinhead' movement, aggressive, often patriotic and racist, which was inner-city, working-class and overwhelmingly male. Paradoxically the skinhead movement was associated with the early arrival of Jamaican reggae in Britain. Skinheads adopted reggae as an antidote to what they saw as the middle-class pretension of 'progressive' music. Similarly, early-70s teenybop pop and glitter rock (Gary Glitter, Bay City Rollers) was adopted largely by teenage girls from the inner cities, while in the same years boys from the suburbs preferred the apparent sophistication of 'pomp rock' (Genesis, Supertramp) and 'glam rock' (Roxy Music, Bowie).

Cities, and especially capital cities, dominate the musical lives of their countries. They are likely to house most music education facilities, record companies, recording studios, national and local radio stations, and concert venues. Provincial cities can also be important, but provincial towns, and especially small towns and rural areas, are far less likely to have any of these facilities; musicians working in these areas are very unlikely to become nationally successful unless they move to one of the metropolitan centres. Liverpool and Manchester have been very important to English pop, but no popular music movement has emerged from the rural areas of England; Country music in the USA is rural in origin but based on the recording studios of Nashville, Tennessee. American bands like Creedence Clearwater Revival are the exceptions which prove the

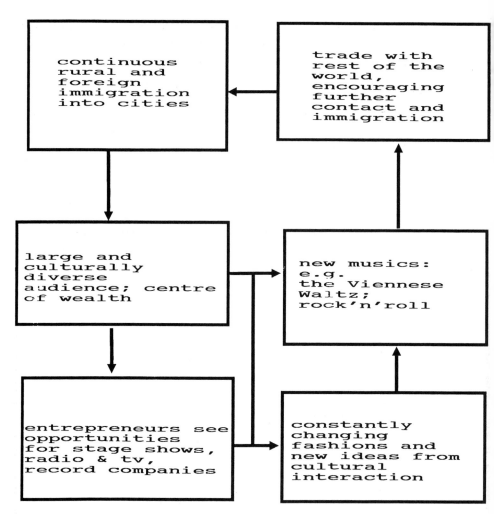

The city and the production of new music.

rule. Popular music worldwide is usually metropolitan music.

Just as important, popular music worldwide is usually American or British and to a lesser extent European. The entertainment industry based on London, Hollywood and New York has dominated the world throughout the century, and continues to do so. American and European domination of entertainment, including the music business, is precisely due to American and European domination of the world economy in other areas. Significantly, the only challenge to this hegemony has been from Japan. But the Japanese challenge in music has so far been restricted to the building and selling of musical instruments and hi-fi systems rather than recordings. No Japanese individual musician or band has done to popular music what Sony (inventor of the Walkman) has done to the world hi-fi market – although Sony's purchase of Columbia (including CBS records) perhaps indicates that they see a future for Japanese musicians as world stars. This is not to suggest that Japanese people are not good musicians, songwriters and record producers. Sadeo Watanabe, for instance, is a widely respected saxophone player, whose recordings sell well in the fusion category which also includes Grover Washington and David Sanborn. But no Japanese singer or band has the world stature of Madonna. The power circuit here is at present balanced between the interests of Japanese and Western capitalism (although the balance is at present moving in Japan's favour). These two interest groups dominate current musical space,

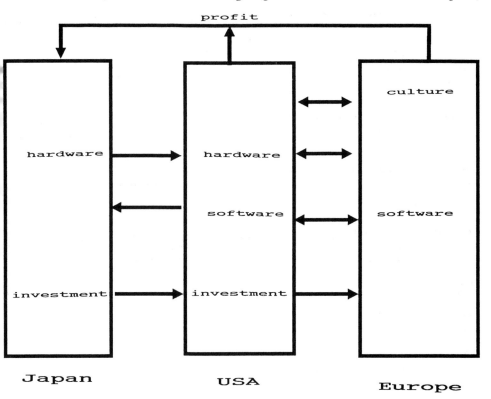

The global music economy, 1991.

and the relations between them are constantly referred to in this book.

Anglo-American and Japanese domination does not mean that other economic relationships in music-making, or other forms of music, have simply ceased to exist. Fears were raised early in the 1970s, as the use of the cassette began to spread through the world, that the music of non-Western cultures would disappear as the young people of the world increasingly listened to Anglo-American pop music recorded in this cheap and easily available format. To a certain extent this has happened. But there are limits to the process, and in many ways it has been reversed. Cassettes also offer a very cheap recording medium, and this has helped local musicians to record their music: the world's record shops are now full of tapes of local music. This is often recorded by major record companies, for local release – by EMI in India for instance. These tapes are bought by tourists, which has created a rising demand for them in Western countries. Specialist labels like Globestyle have helped to establish 'world music' as a thriving category.

The phenomenon of 'world music', which relies on casual exposure to local musics which would be impossible without the cassette, has been a growth industry of recent years, especially in the metropolitan centres. London has many more venues for African and Caribbean music than in 1970; and again this cultural presence offers possibilities for new musical interaction which have already had an impact on the British (and therefore the world) Top 40. So this power circuit is constantly moving music through it in two directions, not simply from the industrial countries to the developing world. Yet in the end the relationship is not balanced. The economic power of the West makes it able to exercise choice, to validate some 'world musics' like central African dance music, and to ignore or reject others (most North African and Middle Eastern musics for instance). This is usually because it is far less familiar to anyone used to Western harmonies and rhythms. Central and West African music is strongly influenced both by the music of the former English or French colonizers and by music from the USA. It is usually sung in English or French, and the harmonies are often familiar, while even if the rhythms are different the basic pulse is still recognizable. North African music, while often as rhythmically exciting as Central or West African music, uses very different harmonies, and is usually sung in Arabic, using the subtle Arabic tradition of vocal and instrumental decoration, which is very strange to Western ears (and of course very beautiful if you're used to it). Cultural imperialism is at work here, in the acceptance of the music of Zaire and Zimbabwe; it is equally at work in the rejection of the music of Morocco and the Sudan. The West is also at best suspicious about, and often hostile to, any cultural form coming from Islam. Although there is a partial exception to this in the popularity of Algerian 'Rai' music in France, a country with past imperial connections with North Africa, and with a large North African population, Rai performers in France were quickly threatened in the early stages of the Gulf War, and many stopped performing in public for a while. Advanced industrial society gives its heartlands, Japan, the United States and Europe, the power to choose; it denies that choice to the satellite countries of the world economy.

The power to choose

In the end, when we discuss the merits of North or West African music, or jazz versus pop, or pop versus rock, or whether we prefer Pat Benatar to Tina Turner, we might say it's all a matter of 'taste'. We like or don't like something – but this taste is formed by our place in the world and the ways we like to use music to assert our own identities. There are many considerations beyond individual preference involved in the acceptance or rejection of musical styles. It is undoubtedly the case that people buy heavy metal albums, or singles by New Kids on the Block, because they like them. It can't be denied that music gives people genuine pleasure. But this is not *simply* a matter of *individual* choice. If we were the only people who liked New Kids on the Block, we wouldn't be able to buy their singles, because there wouldn't be any. Record companies only make records they think they can sell to large numbers of people.

This is not to say that only sure-fire hits are released. Most records are failures. But the music on even these failed products is almost always easy to fit into a category the record industry is happy with: dance music, heavy metal, and so on. Record companies wish to sell to large sectors of the public with similar tastes. Conveniently, such sectors do exist. Taste is never held completely in common, but always articulated in groupings, within categories such as age, class, ethnic identity and gender. These are not exclusive categories: class, ethnic and gender identities do not *determine* what we like. But they tend to offer us exposure to some musics rather than others. Jamaicans are likely to hear reggae and its associated forms (ragamuffin, lover's rock, dance hall and so on). People living in Jamaican communities in, say, London or New York are likely to form peer-groups which listen to and discuss reggae music. They will share experiences of local clubs, PAs and DJs, the latest records and the reggae charts. Middle-class Englishmen are likely to have some exposure to classical music at school; here and at work their peer-groups will listen to and discuss classical music. They will share experiences of concerts and operas, swap recordings and intelligence gathered from magazines. Older people will often listen to the records they bought as teenagers or young adults. They will swap recordings, read and write fanzines, and go to gigs by the middle-aged artists from their youth who have survived: James Brown, the Kinks, or even Engelbert Humperdinck.

Teenage girls will often form fan clubs for the latest pretty young boy pop star, and travel to his gigs together. Swapping recordings, reading magazines, they will operate as a part of a large group centred on common consumer interests, with all the power that gives, often for the only time in their lives. (As a general guide to taste this kind of generalization is useful, but it isn't a rule. Not all Jamaicans prefer Bob Marley to Mantovani. Not all middle-aged blacks prefer Stevie Wonder to Soul II Soul. Not all middle-class men prefer Bach to Bomb the Bass. Not all teenage girls think Jason Donovan is more appealing than Phil Collins).

And yet you *are* more likely to go for New Kids on the Block if you're a young teenage girl than if you're a middle-aged man, and the music business is only able to work because large groups do share the same tastes. Indeed, as far as it can it helps to reinforce these collective tastes, providing publicity material and carefully grooming 'stars' for what it sees as specific markets: providing heavy metal bands like Whitesnake for teenage white boys, rap acts like Public Enemy for teenage blacks, and somehow keeping the Rolling Stones going for middle-aged rock fans. The music business hardly ever tries to create a public taste. I once met a young singer whose record company controlled his diet, regularly took him to the hairdresser, and instructed him to read the London *Times* (so that he would have something interesting to say at interviews!). But the whole point of this particular grooming exercise was to make him look and sound like someone else (Green Gartside, of Scritti Politti).

This record company was trying to respond to consumer demand. It saw that there was a market for soft-voiced, articulate and politically aware singers, and it tried to manufacture one. Similarly, when Bananarama first topped the charts several record companies signed girl singing groups in an attempt to replicate their success. As with my friend Mr Not-Green, it didn't generally work. The practice continued in 1987, when the success of Tracey Chapman, Tanita Tikaram and others led record company executives to look out for female singer-songwriters.

The major companies were not responsible for all that success in the first place: Tanita Tikaram's first album was recorded for a small label run by drummer, producer and songwriter Peter van Hoek. Major multinational entertainment companies like EMI and CBS are depressingly bad at backing new directions in music. Much of punk remained on small labels. This has been especially true in England. The 'progressive' English rock of the late 1960s was mainly on independent labels like Island and Charisma. Decca rejected the Beatles in 1962 (although to be fair they signed the Rolling Stones). However, the situation in America has always been more fluid. CBS reacted quickly to the appearance of progressive rock, signing acts such as Janis Joplin, Blood Sweat and Tears, Santana, Chicago, and even the experimental English band Soft Machine, within a year of their decision to back the new music. The teen-aged Prince was backed to the hilt by Warner Brothers, even through a couple of failed single releases.

The power to use

Why did they do this? What is the motivation behind the record industry's backing of its artists? The basic answer is that they have legal agreements with the artists which will make them a lot of money, if the artists are successful. The power relationships at work here are very complex, involving questions of ownership and obligation which are set out in contracts. Artists will sign contracts firstly with *managers* (who promise to administer their careers so that the artists can spend as much time as possible making music rather than discussing business matters). Usually through the manager's contacts with other people in the business, artists will then sign further contracts with *agents* (who promise to obtain work, including gigs and record deals), *publishers* (who publish sheet music if appropriate, and promise to obtain exposure for the artist's songs and other compositions, and collect royalty payments on them) and *record companies* (who provide the finance to make singles, albums and videos, and market these products). Contracts are legally binding documents, which run for a period of time or for a number of record releases – a record company may wish to sign an artist for 'five albums' rather than five years.

Where there are legal documents, there are also legal disputes, and music lawyers usually wear the satisfied smiles of people who have made the right career decision. Disputes can arise among any combination of the parties who have signed contracts. Certainly in the 1960s many managers, publishers and record companies with a good head for business made exploitative agreements with artists who knew nothing about the law or their own earning possibilities. Their position of power was challenged in the courts. A series of court cases in the UK in the 1970s questioned the publishers' ability to impose their own terms on young songwriters. The courts finally decided that it simply wasn't lawful for publishers to buy large interests in songwriters' future work without making any substantial investment themselves.

The most important case was that of Elton John versus Dick James Music. James had signed John and lyricist Bernie Taupin for £50 each, plus £15 and £10 per week respectively, for which John

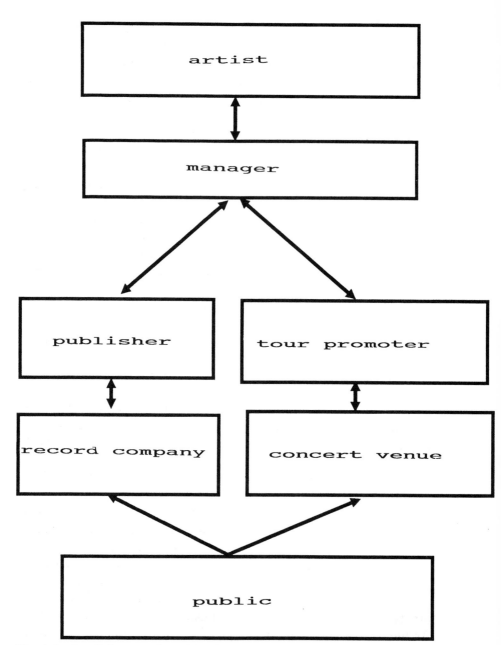

The chain of profit between the artist and the public.

and Taupin were obliged to write at least 18 songs a year for three years. James had gone on to act as John's manager, and his record company, DJM, released Elton John albums. The royalties offered to the artist were paltry: 2 per cent rising to 4 per cent, when the industry average was a hardly generous 12 per cent. The dispute ended with a partial victory for John and Taupin. More importantly, it reinforced the realization within the industry that young artists should be told to seek independent legal advice before signing contracts. This is now the normal procedure, so power relationships within the money-earning structures have changed dramatically as a result of the continuing success of pop and rock acts.

The John versus James dispute was above all about copyright, the single most important way in which money is earned from music. Any broadcast performance of a recorded song or other piece of music means that a royalty payment is due to the owners of copyright in the song, and in the recording. Royalties are collected by companies like the Performing Rights Society and the Mechanical Protection Society and passed to the publisher and record company, who then pay an agreed percentage to the artist. This means that owners of copyrights in successful songs can make fortunes. Dick James sold the Beatles' Northern Songs catalogue to Granada, who auctioned it. The catalogue is now owned by Michael Jackson (who outbid Paul McCartney). Every time you hear 'Yesterday' on the radio, therefore, you can relax in the knowledge that it's helping to keep Michael Jackson in shape. McCartney, meanwhile, was said to be deeply unhappy about the sale, and has since quarrelled with Jackson over the use of the song 'Revolution' in a jeans advertisement.

The power of copyright to earn is not static. Changes in ownership, and in the law, are paralleled by changes in the capital structure of the industry, in music technology, and in the position of the broadcasting industry. Chapter Four will deal with some of these changes in greater detail, but we should note here that the balance of power within the contract circuit is constantly changing. The power of the artist increases with success, often to the point where he or she can dictate his or her own terms. The power of the record label or publisher will also depend on the size and success of the organization. A small label will have less power in the market place, and also less power over the artist, than a major company.

As always, there is no single model for the relationship between artists and the rest of the music business. The Monkees and the Archies, the manufactured groups of the 1960s, may be the model the business is most comfortable with, but it is not the only one. Power does not only rest with the record companies, publishers and agents. Elton John was naive in signing so much of his earning potential over to Dick James, but when John became successful he was able to revenge himself through the courts. Malcolm McLaren and the Sex Pistols took three record labels for a very expensive ride before settling down to shock the world in 1976 with 'Anarchy in the UK'. Sigue Sigue Sputnik took a great deal of advance money, were hyped up by massive advance publicity, and made a couple of records nobody wanted to buy. Meanwhile Frank Zappa continues to make precisely the music he wants to make (23 albums at the last count), owns all his own copyrights, and licenses his work to record labels on his own terms. Power *can* reside with the artist, and with the consumer, who helped John and Zappa to their positions of power, and gave a decisive thumbs down to Sigue Sigue Sputnik.

Technological and legal changes in the structure of the industry are also changing the balance of power. In the UK, and more generally in Europe, in the 1990s, broadcasting is becoming more open. More radio channels are open for commercial broadcasting in Britain; this means that the power to exclude some and include others formerly wielded by the BBC has been ended by the licensing of a series of radio stations dedicated to 'off-centre' programming such as jazz or dance music while, paradoxically, satellite TV has made Europe-wide marketing strategies a possibility. Finally we should note that the advent of the sampler and its associated musical forms has meant that the whole question of copyright has become the most intriguing problem for the industry – one which may well destroy it in its present form.

As always, the consumer figures as a constant, providing the feedback which results in some artists failing, and some going on to successful careers. Consumers and record companies are also in a power relationship which is not simply a one-way system. But it is not a direct relationship. In between lie the media – television, radio, newspapers and magazines – which provide information about new records and videos, and the people who make them. The information provided by the media forms the basis on which most people choose what to listen to and what to buy. They provide the information in a number of different ways. Papers like *Melody Maker* and *Rolling Stone* concentrate on album and video reviews, and interviews with a wide range of performers and producers. Other magazines cater for special interests: jazz, teen-age stars and chart hits, soul, hip-hop, and so on. But most newspapers concern themselves with popular music in some way or other. The London *Times* signalled the coming of age of the first rock music generation by appointing former *Melody Maker* editor Richard Williams to the post of rock critic in the early 1970s. The *Times*'s sister paper, the down-market tabloid the *Sun*, on the other hand, signalled the problems of rock stardom when it mounted a hate campaign against Elton John in the late 1980s, publishing a series of scurrilous accusations about the singer-songwriter's sex life. This culminated in a libel lawsuit which John won, forcing the *Sun* to pay £1 million in damages.

Radio stations can also dish the dirt – but more importantly they provide the blanket coverage of music which the record industry needs. What they do not do is give equal coverage to every release. In England, the power of the BBC in 'playlisting' the singles most likely to make the Top 40 (and ignoring most of the others) has begun to decline, largely because this policy did not serve the market. The 1980s were a decade in which illegal 'pirate' radio stations flourished in the bigger British cities – by playing music ignored by the BBC. This was usually music the BBC claimed to 'belong' to a minority ethnic community (including jazz, fusion, funk, soul, hip-hop, reggae and other black musics; bhangra and other Indian disco music; Greek and Turkish popular music; but also other forms the BBC saw as minority-interest, such as early-1970s 'album rock' and heavy metal). Recent legislation has opened up the airwaves a little, and the situation in Britain in the 1990s is more like that in the USA. The development of music radio in the United States, which has always been commercial and market-led, has allowed a very large number of radio stations catering for a wider variety of tastes, ages (from childhood to retirement), and ethnic groups, through a fluid set of categories such as Album-Oriented Rock, Urban Contemporary (marketing managers' latest name for black music without using the word black, still offensive in some parts of racist America), Contemporary Hit Radio, Gold (old hits), Gospel, and more recently the rather similar New Age and Quiet Storm among many others.

But perhaps the most important form of exposure to the public is via television. By the early 1960s it was being seen as the most important means of promotion. Record companies and artists' managers tried to place their protégés both on chat shows and on dedicated pop music shows like *Ready, Steady Go* and *Top of the Pops* in Britain and *Soul Train* in the USA. A major change in the method of promotion worldwide since the early 1980s has been the increased reliance on the promotional video as much as on live public performance. This has led to a new television format. The phenomenal Stateside success of MTV, based since its inception in 1982 on the very simple format of the non-stop broadcasting of pop videos, has led to similar channels all over Europe, such as British Sky Broadcasting's own version of MTV. Here again there are restrictions in coverage, most obviously the deliberate racism of early American MTV programming. Soul and hip-hop was ignored in the early years of MTV, despite mounting criticism from white artists among many others. The first black person to appear regularly on MTV was Michael Jackson. The worldwide success of *Thriller* simply could not be ignored, but black artists, and especially black artists not yet established, are still under-repre-sented on MTV.

One more mediating form between consumer and record industry should be noted. There has been a significant growth in recent years in the field of contemporary cultural studies, and popular music has become a respectable subject of academic study. Books and journals about popular music are published from all the major European and American educational institutions. Some people would see this as irrelevant to producers and consumers alike. Whether for good or ill, however, academic critics are not simply forgettable figures lan-guishing in ivory towers. They help to train teachers, and also future journalists, and workers for radio and television companies. The British music press of the 1970s and 1980s was deeply influenced by university-taught theories of cultural politics and semiotics, influenced in other words by writers such as Marx, Freud, Marcuse, Barthes and Foucault. Music critics can be powerful and influential people: their opinions can help to make or break a new recording act. Theory can be powerful. Furthermore, the work of these theor-ists is increasingly being taught on music courses, and therefore helps to train future musicians. Therefore, cultural theories about the place of music in society are important, even if they are 'wrong'. (Wrong or right, the theorists are always people with a cultural place of their own. Most academic writers on music, like the present one, are white middle-class males with some musical experience.)

Academic criticism attempts to find meanings in music by using one or more of a number of approaches. Firstly, there is straightfor-ward analysis of the *production* of music: the decisions made by musicians and record companies, the writing, recording and market-ing of music. Secondly there are analyses of the *meanings* of songs or other pieces of music: these can be examinations of lyrics, or more sophisticated attempts to appreciate the uses of rhythm, har-mony, melody, instrumentation and the structures and conventions of songs. Thirdly, there are cultural analyses which look at the *uses* of music by fractions of the public. These examine the place of music in youth culture and especially youth subcultures, and attempt to address the important questions of class, ethnic and gender identity among people who share musical tastes but often differ in social backgrounds. Although there are problems with all these ways of seeing music, taken together they represent a wide variety of approaches which help musicians and admirers of music alike to understand the ways in which music works as a system of communication. All these approaches have informed the writing of this book; readers wishing to explore the ideas behind them in more detail should consult the Further Reading list (p. 126).

3 Inside the circuit: making music

Performing musicians have to confront and negotiate with all these questions of power on a day-to-day basis. This chapter looks at the ways in which music is performed, and some of the cultural and economic constraints which surround musical performance. Power in music is most immediately confronted by the performer firstly in his or her education. Chapter five deals in more detail with questions of education, but we should note here that this doesn't just mean the learning of instrumental or vocal technique, but also learning the possibilities offered to the musician by his or her cultural tradition. The place of that education and culture in the world's power system will then determine the availability of opportunities for various kinds of music making.

Music and performance is placed differently in different cultures. Some cultures insist that music should be subject to commercial considerations, others that it be subordinate to religious expression. Some cultures deny women any opportunity to become musicians; others ensure that women musicians do not perform in public. Until very recently most European orchestras followed this cultural practice of excluding women: the world famous Vienna Philharmonic Orchestra still excludes women. Newly developed performance, broadcast and recording technologies are no different in this respect from orchestras, or any other set of human musical activities. Access to any technologies will only be available to people with cultural as well as economic power, and once again women have been systematically pressured by Western culture away from certain forms of musicianship and composition. They have also been excluded from the power hierarchies of the music business. There are for instance no female directors of London-based record companies. This exclusion is not maintained on the basis of skills or abilities, but culture: 'custom and practice', a power circuit which in this case continues to devalue and exclude female musicianship.

Any culture, in fact, contains within it hierarchies of opportunity for music-making, which are denied to some members of the culture, and to members of many other cultures. Most obviously, people from poorer countries and social classes, and disadvantaged ethnic, religious and gender groups within wealthy countries, have less access to these opportunities, although disadvantage is seldom absolute; the cultural boundaries within which music is made are always being redrawn. Black American music from hip-hop onwards has made music from cheap technology – and this music is

The end of a learning process: trumpeter Mark Isham in performance.

now successful worldwide, turning many of those who make it into wealthy star performers. Similarly, while jazz and blues have been the music of the oppressed, they have also been ways in which individual musicians could break clear of the ghetto and live the American Dream. (There have also been dominant cultures which have encouraged the musicianship of the groups they dominated, as for example gypsies in eastern Europe; and cultures which have musician-castes within them, people who are literally born into musicianship, such as the *iggawin* in Mauritania.)

Less obvious but equally important restraints operate against young people from the middle class who wish to become professional musicians in popular music. Popular music is still not seen as a respectable profession with guaranteed rewards in the same ways as medicine, the law or accountancy, and parents and careers advisers are often hostile to any young person who wishes to make a career solely from music. Nevertheless, entering the profession of music requires capital: opportunities to play expensive instruments, to record and so on are only available to those who can pay, or who can find a sponsor.

Social groups without access to instruments are far more likely to make music which doesn't need them. 'Do-wop' close harmony singing in the 1950s was a musical form in which groups of young black American men and women made music without the expense of instruments. Hip-hop, likewise, is music of the street, developed by underprivileged blacks; based on the voice, the cheap drum machine and the turntable, it does not use the sophisticated instruments of, say, jazz-funk (a.k.a 'fusion'), a music preferred by many wealthier blacks – who can afford to buy and learn expensive instruments like guitars, keyboards and saxophones.

It's worth developing this contrast here. Jazz-funk is a sophisticated musical form, with many accepted rules of harmony, melody and rhythm, and conventions of improvisation, which have to be learned alongside the bodily disciplines of a particular instrument. To play the saxophone, or the trumpet, needs physical fitness for breath control and stamina, as well as the training of the ear and mouth to play 'in tune' with other instruments. This is a complex business, which needs dedication and time, and unsurprisingly many of the best players of this form are college-trained musicians. To become a respected jazz-funk player requires the same as any other form of jazz: hard work, a period of learning before public performance, and an apprenticeship as a sideman in someone else's band.

On the face of it, hip-hop is an easier proposition altogether. And yet hip-hop is also a learned style, with its own codes of musicality and meaning; codes which like those of jazz-funk involve the rela-

Mantronix. A different set of performance practices are in play here; although they still have to be learnt.

tionship between the body and technology. The performance of any music is a learned bodily discipline – whether it be playing the saxophone or scratching a turntable. Even singing is not natural or given, but has to be learned, from specific cultural traditions and reference points – whether it be from formal singing lessons or copying from records. Yet singing again almost always involves the relationship of the body with performing technology. Microphones, amplifiers and reverberation and delay units aid vocal performances of all sorts outside the church and the opera house. Making all other kinds of music requires some interaction between the body and music technology.

While musicians learn to perform within a given technology, they often find the limits of the technology they use unsatisfactory, and their demands and expectations then help to fuel the further development of these technologies. Innovation in music technology has a complex relationship with changing relations of economic and cultural power as well as with changing composition and performance styles and possibilities. We have already noticed the strong relationship between cultural dominance, technological innovation and the organization of capital. By the end of the seventeenth century, the revival of interest in the Classical civilizations of Greece and Rome which started in the fourteenth century Italian Renaissance had spread all over Europe. Italy was seen as the centre of European culture, and Italian aesthetics (ideas about what was beautiful) influenced art and architecture all over Europe. Buildings from St Petersburg in Russia to London's St Paul's Cathedral were styled under the Italian influence. Italy was also seen as the home of music. The language of classical music – words like concerto, opera, aria, finale and so on – remain largely Italian. The cultural hegemony of Italian aesthetics was matched by the power and influence of the trading city-states like Genoa and especially Venice, the latter dominating the Meditteranean. This was also the age of the craft workshop: the lack of power resources other than water and muscles meant that most manufacture was on a small scale. The manufacture of any complex item from furniture to cannon was carried out by master craftsmen with small teams of assistants and apprentices. Italian craftsman-built stringed instruments were in demand all over Europe. Even today, violins made by the workshops of Amati and Stradivarius remain the most valuable of all musical investments: so valuable that many are kept in secure storage, and therefore cannot fulfil their original function as musical instruments.

But by the middle of the nineteenth century the craft workshop was no longer the dominant mode of production. The conquest and settling of the New World led to the increasing importance of

A seventeenth-century violin before restoration. Violins are still made; the design of the instrument has hardly changed. (Photo courtesy of the Victoria and Albert Museum)

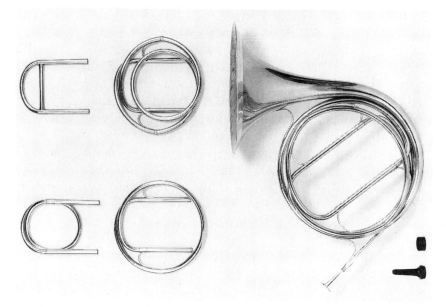

Victorian high technology: the coming of the valve.
A: An early nineteenth-century horn, with the different lengths of tubing or 'crooks'
the player needed to use in order to play in different keys.
B: A cornet of about 1830. Here the different lengths of tubing are already attached,
and the player merely has to open and close them through the three valves at the top
of the instrument. (Photos courtesy of the Victoria and Albert Museum)

countries trading with America. Countries opening on to the Atlantic, and especially Britain and Holland, became increasingly wealthy, and started to develop new forms of power resource like steam from coal-burning: the process known as the 'industrial revolution' began. By the beginning of the nineteenth century the industrial revolution had moved cultural and economic dominance to northern Europe, and there followed a revival in Gothic architecture, which had been the building style of northern Europe in the middle ages. This cultural dominance also found expression in the novel, a new way of writing about contemporary people, which was developed in Britain and France above all. Where even in the late eighteenth century the Austrian Mozart wrote music which owed a lot to Italian models, nineteenth-century German composers like Beethoven, Schumann and Brahms wrote confidently in a style they thought was quite specifically German. There were also northern European innovations in music technology. The saxophone was invented in Belgium in 1840, and valve-action brass band instruments (trumpet, horn and tuba) and keyed woodwind instruments (the 'Boehm system' flute and clarinet) were developed in France, Germany and Great Britain. Methods of manufacture had changed. Craftsman Adolphe Saxe developed the saxophone from the clarinet, a 'woodwind' instrument, but it was made from brass, with complex metal keywork which could be machine-made. The valve-action brass band instruments in particular were genuine products of the industrial revolution, mass-produced in factories rather than built by hand. They were therefore cheaper and available to more people than craftsman-produced stringed instruments. The brass band movement of nineteenth century Britain was largely working class because of the availability of instruments.

This was a development of available resources, not simply a replacement. The violin did not disappear. People still learned to play it, and craftsmen still learned to make it, as they continue to do today. But it reached its optimum size in the seventeenth century, and apart from some strengthening of the bow, the lengthening of the fingerboard, and the introduction of new materials for making strings (metals and plastics to replace the traditional gut), the violin and the other classical stringed instruments have not developed since. The more mechanical brass and wind instruments of the industrial revolution, on the other hand, are continually being 'improved'; the mechanics of the keywork, and the metals used to make them, are always in flux, while the precise placing of the holes and keys are continually being refined according to the principles of acoustics and the changing demands of performers for harder or more mellow sounds. New instruments like the contrabass clarinet

Virtuoso performer Harry Sparnay playing the contrabass clarinet, another example of Victorian keywork technology, now much improved by twentieth-century acoustic design.

have been developed from the smaller forms in the twentieth century because metal technology and knowledge of acoustics has made their manufacture possible. Unlike violins, however, brass and wind instruments do not improve with age.

In the twentieth century, and especially since the Second World War, dominance first resided in the United States, the great world economic and cultural power of the 30 years from 1945. The electric guitar and bass guitar, and the earliest multitrack recording systems, were developed in the USA in the 1950s. Amplification systems for 'stadium rock' concerts were developed after the mass popularity of Elvis, and tours in the early 1960s by British bands such as the Beatles, the Rolling Stones and Herman's Hermits, signalled the need for them. As well as the electric guitar, a development of an existing instrument, and Leo Fender's development of the bass guitar, America saw the first completely new volume-produced instruments since the nineteenth century. The Hammond Organ, using a new system of sound generation, was introduced in the 1940s. In the late 1960s the Moog synthesizer appeared. Again, this used a new electronic system of sound production. Vibrating 'oscillators' are changed in pitch by raising and lowering the voltage put through them. This basic sound can then be combined with the products of other oscillators, and/or put through electric circuits which filter, delay or distort the sound.

Before the development of the integrated circuit or microchip, these electronic instruments were bulky and unreliable. The first

Erasure pose with an early synthesizer. It's clearly built for the studio.

Moog synthesizer was a colossal and very expensive assembly which needed time and dedication to use effectively: but its sound was popularized by supergroups like Emerson, Lake and Palmer, and within a few years the portable (and much more affordable) Minimoog was providing bass lines and solos in live bands and on record. The Minimoog's success prompted many other companies to make small synthesizers. These instruments were *monophonic* – only able to play one note at a time. The earliest *polyphonic* synthesizers (able to play several notes simultaneously) were also developed in the USA, by Moog, Oberheim and Sequential Circuits among others. These were all small, independent high-tech companies based in centres like Silicon Valley, and while their corporate structure allowed them to innovate and develop ideas easily, their small scale prevented genuine mass production and worldwide marketing so their products remained relatively expensive. In many ways these companies were operating like the craft workshops which made stringed instruments in seventeenth-century Italy. This small-scale innovation continues: a recent example is the Chapman Stick, which looks like a minimalist electric guitar, but calls for a very different playing technique. Emmett Chapman makes the instruments himself, as Leo Fender did in the early years of the Fender guitar company.

But in the early 1980s, even as the Sequential Circuits Prophet 5 and Prophet 10 were becoming the synthesizers played on every album, and the instruments everyone wanted to own, the American dominance of capital and innovation was being challenged by Japan. Japanese music companies like Korg, Roland and Yamaha made perfectly decent-sounding polyphonic synthesizers in the late 1970s, and made them more cheaply by mass producing them. However, innovation remained largely a European and American prerogative until the appearance of the Yamaha DX7 synthesizer in 1983 signalled the rise to dominance of Japanese computer-based technologies. The DX7 was the first digital synthesizer affordable by more than the wealthiest musicians. Its digital technology replaced the oscillators of the conventional synthesizer with microchips dedicated to turning chains of numbers into sound. The crucial point here is that the method of sound creation used by the DX7, FM digital synthesis, was the development of an idea produced by an American academic and composer, John Chowning. No American company would back the development of this system for mass production. Yamaha took the project on, did all the necessary commercial development, and still profits from the decision through its current generation of digital synthesizers, the SY series, which has added to the FM system and made it easier to program.

The Minimoog, the first popular and reliable portable synthesizer.

The Micromoog, even more compact (and cheaper) than the Minimoog.

The two other great sound-producing innovations of the 1980s tell a similar story. In 1981 the worldwide MIDI specification was agreed by the American and Japanese electronic musical instrument manufacturers, meeting under the chairmanship of the American inventor Dave Smith. MIDI stands for Musical Instrument Digital Interface. It is an interface which allows computers, electronic musical instruments like synthesizers, and other musical devices, to be connected together by a simple cable. Using MIDI, synthesizers can

Emmett Chapman plays his own invention, the Stick.

control each other; computers can be programmed to control both synthesizers, and other compatible devices like reverberation and delay units and mixing desks. A computer program which controls MIDI instruments (called a sequencing program, or sequencer) makes the computer act as a kind of tape recorder, storing the information played into it from an instrument and then making the instrument repeat the original information at will. The other innovation is the sampler, a device which uses computer memory to record sound in digital form. The recorded or 'sampled' sound (any sound – a car horn, say) can then be manipulated, and via MIDI, played from a keyboard, or controlled by a sequencer. The combination of sampler and sequencer produced a powerful new type of musical instrument in the mid-1980s: House music and its variants would have been impossible without this combination.

The first commercial sampling and sequencing systems were produced by the Australian company Fairlight Instruments and by the American Synclavier, which also used a form of FM synthesis. These were ground-breaking machines, but difficult to use and very expensive. Although several American companies then produced cheaper sampling systems, they tended to work at lower resolution (they were quite noisy, and samples of high-frequency sounds like cymbals sounded dull). They were also, still, difficult to operate: the Ensoniq Mirage was affordable by semi-professional and hobby musicians in the West, but its operating system was built for competent mathematicians only. The first company to come up with an affordable sampler offering both high resolution, and a user-friendly operating system (even printing the word 'oops!' on the screen when you made a mistake, but more importantly telling you what to do about it), was the Japanese company Akai with the S900. Akai now dominate world sales of sampling systems.

The dominance of Japanese capital has not been absolute, however. This is again partly due to the continuing ability of American and European companies to innovate. The development of the MIDI

The Yamaha DX7, probably the most popular professional musical instrument of the 1980s. Despite this it is fearsomely difficult to program, something more recent Yamaha instruments have tried to overcome.

specification offered immediate possibilities for new integrated recording and sequencing devices like the Fairlight, and for the control of synthesizers in live performance. It also offered new possibilities for the use of existing home and desktop microcomputers. American computer systems, especially the Apple Macintosh, the Atari ST and the IBM PC, have been very important in the development of integrated computer-based recording systems. European (especially German) software for these systems is acknowledged to be among the best in the world. No computer system developed in Japan has yet succeeded in gaining the essential support of musicians, although Yamaha in particular have begun to develop very competitive products in this field. But stage performance instruments (including drums, guitars and brass and wind instruments as well as keyboards) are almost all Japanese, and most of the small, innovative American instrument-makers like Fender Rhodes, Sequential Circuits and Oberheim (as well as the Linn drum-machine company) have either failed or have been bought out by Japanese companies. Meanwhile the Yamaha DX7 became through the mid-1980s the world's most popular high-technology performance instrument. In 1989 a series of eight BBC television programmes, 'Under African Skies', featured music from all over Africa. Among the many different percussion instruments, brass, and guitars, the DX7 appeared on all the programmes, as the only electronic performance keyboard in popular music groups from Ethiopia to South Africa. Japan is now the dominant centre of capital development in music technology, as in so many other areas of microprocessor-based electronics, and this success is based on providing relatively inexpensive instruments which people actually want to play.

Here, as much as in the case of the record-buying public, the power to use and choose remains important. The performing musician as a consumer is an active rather than a passive figure. Throughout history musicians and composers have helped the development of the instruments they use to perform. The fingerboard of the violin was extended in the nineteenth century to provide more high notes for virtuosi like Paganini. Keys were added to wind instruments, and valves to brass instruments, to help performers play 'in tune' in the 'diatonic' system (harmony based on twelve equal divisions of the octave) which was accepted all over Europe by the middle of the eighteenth century. The design of the piano was radically changed through the nineteenth century as composer/performers like Beethoven, Chopin and Liszt demanded greater volume and flexibility of tone. In more recent times players have demanded (and obtained) synthesizers with more responsive keyboards, more 'user-friendly' programming for samplers and synthesizers, and different ways of controlling synthesizers such as guitar, wind and percussion-based controllers as well as keyboards. Composers and songwriters have helped with the development of microcomputer based sampling, recording and sequencing systems: Frank Zappa even insists on taking his Synclavier on tour with his live bands, and musicians as different as Kate Bush and Barry Manilow have paid tribute to the helpfulness of computer-based systems in songwriting.

Yet as with all relationships within the power circuit, the relationship between performance technology and performer are never the

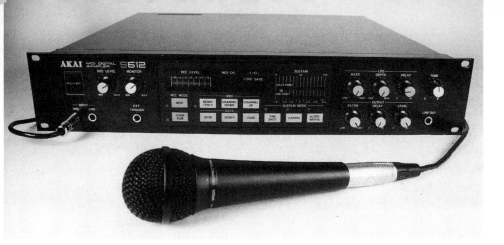

An early Akai sampler, the S612, compact and 'affordable'.

Confirmation of the current dominance of Japanese capital. Roger Linn used to make drum machines of his own. Akai liked them so much, they bought the company, and Mr Linn now designs Akai products – in this case a rather unreliable sampling drum machine.

straightforward one of a responsive industry simply providing what the performer wants. Performing technology is never perfect, and it is not always 'progressive'; many developments impose restrictions on the performer which were not imposed by previous, simpler instruments. The diatonic system of the mid-eighteenth century 'well-tempered' keyboard, and the following developments in wind and brass instruments, made those instruments far less flexible in the subtle and expressive variations in pitch which are still taken for granted in many Asian and African musics. There is often a similar loss of flexibility in computer-sequenced music. Many very expensive drum machines and computer-based sequencing devices available in the mid-1980s, including the £60,000 Fairlight Series III music computer, were designed to play Western pop music, which uses only a very few basic rhythms. They were unable to play either in complex time signatures or even in the more subtle variations within the basic rhythms such as 'swing' or 'shuffle' time. Music played into these devices would be automatically corrected to the nearest beat or subdivided beat (in the computer's opinion!). This led to a lot of popular music sounding very mechanical and robotic. The complaints of performers, producers and listeners led to the development of more subtle devices within computer software (often with names like 'groove factor' or 'human touch'), which have largely solved this problem either by randomly altering some of the data in the computer's memory, or by allowing the user to override the computer's strict sense of rhythmic accuracy. Computer programmers are thus opening up new opportunities for human performance once again.

Many problems remain with this approach to music-making, however quick the hardware and software companies are to develop

A home keyboard of the 1790s: the square fortepiano. (Photo courtesy of the Victoria and Albert Museum)

The public 'concert' version, an early nineteenth-century grand piano. In this instance, while modern instruments look very similar, in fact they are far more rugged in construction, thanks to the demands of concert performers like Liszt. (Photo courtesy of the Victoria and Albert Museum)

products in response to the demands of producers, performers and composers. At present all such systems have to be learnt fairly intensively. While few machines today (1992) are as complex to learn as the first Mirage, users of these devices have to develop very high general skills in computer literacy, and specific skills to operate each device, *as well as* traditional musical skills of instrumental or vocal technique and composition. An example of this type of literacy and its complexities is seen in the page reproduced on p. 59 from the magazine *Home & Studio Recording*. This is a review of a piece of sound-editing software for the Roland D110 synthesizer module. The software package only runs on an Atari ST computer. Someone wishing to use the D110 will need, as well as the computer, at least either a further software package for sequencing and composing, or for live use a keyboard or other MIDI controller, each of which will use another set of commands. Furthermore, each software package arranges the screen in a different way, as these examples show. Clearly in the ideal world several sets of control commands have to be learnt before a note of music can be played.

In practice, most people using music technology learn as little as possible. The pattern of product replacement is now such that new machines with claimed superiority of performance appear from each major Japanese manufacturer on a two-year basis. Software packages are more usually upgraded every few months. This doesn't encourage professional users to spend a great deal of time learning to use the full capabilities of devices which they know will soon be replaced. Secondly, since devices like the D110 have many built-in 'pre-set' sounds, most users will take one shortcut by using only the pre-sets, and will never learn how to edit the internal sound-producing structure. So another common restriction in the performance of popular music is the continuing reappearance of the same pre-set sounds (a week before writing this, I heard some over-familiar Yamaha pre-set sounds on a broadcast of a Madonna concert). The enormous potential of these machines for original sounds is hardly ever realized.

Clearly in some ways there is a conflict here between the economic interests of the instrument developer and the musical needs of

The ultimate performer's and composer's keyboard instrument, the Synclavier music computer.

the performer. The instrument maker wants to develop the most sophisticated product offering the best sound and the most sophisticated facilities for manipulating sound. Competition between manufacturers means that new instruments are launched regularly. In many ways this benefits the performer. The manufacture and programming of microchips is essentially cheap; the pace of innovation and competition ensures that one year's flagship facilities will be available on the next year's budget models. But the performer also wants something which is reliable and easy to use, and to learn to use. Programming newer instruments is more difficult partly because fewer editing controls are offered to the user. Older synthesizers like the Prophet 5, or the Prophet 10 illustrated on p. 62, provided the user with an array of electromechanical devices like panpots and sliders, each of which controlled a single editing function, for instance the length of decay on a note after the key has been released. Each of these controls is as expensive as many microchips. Typically if you want to create or edit a sound using a more recent digital synthesizer, individual areas of performance like timbre, filtering, tuning, length of attack and decay and so forth have to be addressed and altered one at a time through a single 'window'. This simplicity of facility keeps the price down, but makes the instruments time-consuming to prepare – hence the need for editing software – and this makes them especially inflexible in live performance. Many synthesizers discarded by their makers in the name of

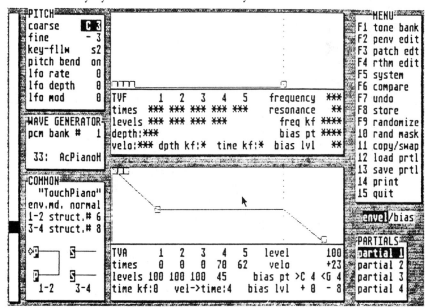

A typical piece of music software, in this case an editing program for the Roland D110 synthesizer.

'progress' (such as the Minimoog, the ARP Oddysey, the Roland Super Jupiter) have remained in demand as classic instruments, partly because their analogue sound-producing system produces sounds unique to them, and partly because their control layout makes them easier to program. They have separate slider controls for every aspect of sound creation and control. The multi-language problem which has to be conquered in order to use the D110 does not exist in this case. Acid House music in particular revived a demand for synthesizers which could be reprogrammed during performance, opening or closing filters to change the sound of a repeated bass riff or hi-hat pattern, for example. Ease of use, cheapness and sophistication of facilities remain a problematic opposition.

Even if these problems were solved, the performer and producer are still faced with a number of other problems before music is made. There is the question of what to do about stage performance, which is still important in almost all forms of music as a promotional tool, but distinctly uncharismatic if done to the accompaniment of a tape recorder or sequencer rather than 'live'. That is, assuming the technology actually works on stage. Microtechnology, and especially sequencing systems, are not yet reliable enough to ensure nightmare-free gigs. The weak points are obviously the cable connections. MIDI cables have to be short to work efficiently, which either means everything and everybody being crammed together, or the use of individual performing stations; not much of a help in developing group feel. Mixing the sounds emanating from many synthetic sound sources is a nightmare – it's difficult enough even when you can see drums being hit or trumpets being blown, but when all the sounds come from keyboards or drum machines, identifying their source from many yards away can be virtually impossible. Then there are practical problems associated with computers. Disk drives are delicate, and often give trouble if used for long tours. Power surges or accidents with cables can cause memory loss in computers and sequencers. I am not the only musician who has had to wait embarrassed on stage while a sequence was reloaded into a system which had crashed. Musicians who wish to play 'live' but use computers on stage as a shortcut to musical competence, are advised to practise those guitar licks after all. They may just be needed.

In any case, this is not the only way to make music. Many musicians fear or loathe the computer-based technologies, and do without them altogether. Heavy metal bands, which rely on touring and audience response to sell their products, are by and large synthesizer-free. They share this distaste for high technology (but very little else) with the female singer-songwriters who were so successful in the late

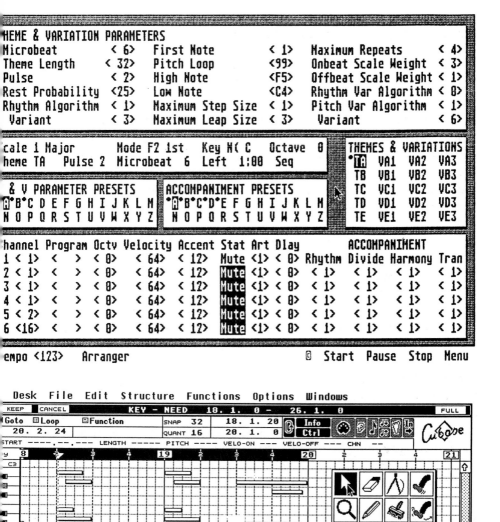

Two popular pieces of music software for the Atari computer.
Below, the Steinberg Cubase sequencing program.

1980s, such as Michelle Shocked, Tracey Chapman and Tanita Tikaram, who were accompanied by traditional instruments rather than batteries of synthesizers and samplers with more flashing lights than moving parts. The worldwide success of Sade in the mid-1980s was in part due to old-fashioned sonic values: the 'live' sounds of bass, guitar, drums and saxophone, without the use of synthesizer or sampler, were the same on tour as on record. Tears for Fears, on world tour in 1990, announced publicly that they had abandoned much of the high-technology of their previous tours, and were using guitars, drums, acoustic piano and so on, played live. The Rolling Stones, still showing themselves to the public in 1990 as in 1964, have always used traditional stage instruments. This is not simply due to the nature of the audience, who would demand a nostalgic night out (i.e. what they are already used to). The recent revival of guitar and drums bands centred on Manchester, England, shows that young people can also play live, and young audiences flock to see them do it, and that in other words traditional 1960s methods of making pop music are valid enough to have worldwide success.

Hopefully I've shown that there is no simple relationship between technological innovation and musical 'progress'. But I don't want to end the discussion by singing the praises of 1960s performing techniques. Even for live performance, certain aspects of high technology are a blessing. In order to see why this is, we have to return to one of the key statements made earlier in the chapter: music is a learned bodily discipline. The physical challenges of musical performance (of making an instrument like a trumpet sound 'nice', or play high notes or low notes successfully; or of playing passages on a keyboard smoothly) give the trained musician pleasure. The

The popular and fairly user-friendly Prophet synethesizer.

Detail of the Roland Jupiter 8's programming controls. Roland have reintroduced these knobs and switches in response to demand for more responsive, less time-consuming programming systems.

pleasures available to the performer have been greatly increased by the possibilities offered by high technology. For the keyboard, guitar, percussion, wind or brass player, MIDI controllers offer whole new ranges of sounds and whole new ways of playing.

It's easy enough to agree that performing gives musicians pleasure. But what about the audience? This, after all, is what gigs of all sorts are about. If musicians simply wanted to play, they could do it in their bedrooms. Many do. This leads to the question: why is public musical performance still so popular in the age of multi-channel television, the video, and general broadcasting success? Why do people want to perform in public, and why does the public want to see performance?

There are several different questions here, with rather different answers. Economically, it continues to be important for musicians to appear in public simply to remind the public of their presence. So even if gigs are expensive to promote, involving PA, lights, video relays and so on, being transported all over the world in many cases, record companies will set them up when a band releases a new album and hope to get their money back from album sales. Heavy losses on tour are often written off against tax, and are therefore worthwhile for big-earning artists and record companies alike. Even so, gigs can be financially supported in many ways. Merchandizing – sales of albums, videos, books, programmes, T-shirts and so on – at the gigs is often more lucrative than ticket sales. Furthermore, support acts usually pay the main band or artist; they will hope to break through into public awareness by supporting a successful act.

The economics are clear enough in the case of major rock and pop acts supported by major record labels. For minority musics there are less compelling financial reasons for live performance. Why do concert pianists, or jazz musicians, endure the discomforts of life 'on the road' when the recording studio allows them to make virtually

The Roland S550 sampler: same company, but far more difficult to use.

perfect recordings of the music of their choice? Why does the owner of an expensive hi-fi and dozens of records by concert pianist Vladimir Ashkenazy or jazz saxophonist Sonny Rollins wish to travel 30 miles to sit in an uncomfortable seat in a concert hall with poor acoustics in order to hear Ashkenazy or Rollins play live? The answer here in both cases is partly the challenge and excitement of playing difficult music live. Concert performances of classical music can be very tense occasions, as the player(s) negotiate passages both they and the listener know are very difficult. There is a shared sense of danger – serious mistakes can be made which can disrupt or spoil the performance. The details of interpretation in live performances are unpredictable. A performer may choose to play a passage more slowly, or more loudly, than she or he does on a particular record. This access to the possibilities of interpretation is also a pleasure shared with the audience. These kinds of pleasures are also present, often in heightened form, in jazz performances. The audience shares the challenges faced by the musician: of improvising around a set of chord changes known to be difficult, and of interacting with other musicians who are also improvising. Both in concert music and jazz, a bad performance, even outright 'failure', is possible: the outcome of the event is impossible to predict.

New instruments often use traditional performing techniques: the author playing soprano saxophone and Akai's EWI, a wind instrument MIDI controller. The fingering for the two instruments is virtually identical. (Photos courtesy of Lesley Crewdson)

Musical performance in this sense, stressing the difficulty and the unpredictability involved, becomes very like sport, and gives similar pleasures. In sporting contests the rules are known to everyone, and the successes and failures of interpretation and improvisation within the contest are shared by performers and audience alike, although as with concert music there is a clear difference between the virtuoso professional performer and the audience. The outcome of the sporting contest is likewise impossible to predict.

This is precisely *not* what the performers or audience are looking for at a concert by Bob Dylan, the Grateful Dead or Barry Manilow (although Dylan has a habit of upsetting the expectations of his fans and playing either new material, or new arrangements of old songs). What is on offer here (and in some 'popular classical' concerts, of music by Tchaikovsky for example) is what some would characterize as 'nostalgia': the performers are expected to play the songs everyone knows, in as familiar a way as possible. In many popular music concerts of this type there are opportunities to sing along with the familiar material, thus diminishing the distance between the performer and the audience in a way which would be impossible with the concert pianist or jazz saxophonist. The outcome should be predictable in both form and content.

And yet there are connections between the audience's experiences, notably the pleasure shared among the members of the audience themselves. They witness the event collectively in a way which is impossible in their homes: in many concerts the audience has a power in its collective form which is impossible for individuals – the 'hysteria' which greets succesive generations of pop stars being the obvious example. The sharing of pleasure at a public event increases the personal pleasure of the individual.

So public performance can raise very different expectations and give very different pleasures. The music can be familiar or unfamiliar; it can challenge ideas and values, or reinforce them. It provides opportunities for the sharing and expression of these values in public, in a way which is impossible within the private domestic pleasures of broadcast media. This collective celebration is not always totally positive. Any form of cultural identification involves the creation of a negative 'other'; the concert gives the opportunity for many forms of cultural snobbery, or even sheer hatred, directed against those who are not present and do not choose to identify with a particular type of music. An obvious example would be heavy metal. The components of this form include music played very loudly by white men; gigs attended mainly by teenage boys and young men; lyrics which treat women as disposable sex objects; women who attend these concerts dressing as sex objects. Clearly

Ian Anderson, of Jethro Tull, a rock band which has been around for over 20 years. The fans will expect to hear the familiar rather than the new.

the entire sequence of events reinforces gender roles: power is masculine, men rule the world; women are incidental, present for men's pleasure, absent from all else. Most heavy metal gigs are just as overbearingly masculine as boardroom meetings at major companies. (Challenges to these stereotypes from all-female bands like Vixen and all-black bands like Living Colour may in time succeed, but are peripheral and in some ways therefore reinforce the stereotypes at present). Most 'teenybop' gigs, by contrast – say, the 1988 tour by Bros – offer opportunities for young girls to get together, form the majority of an audience, and through sharing their emotions display their collective power as consumers. While this type of event also plays around a restrictive version of female sexuality, it is an event which is empowering rather than diminishing to those young women who partake of the collective concert experience.

The effects on the actual performers of teenybop music are contradictory. Economically, success as a pop star will usually be rewarding. Musically, many performers find this particular version of 'success' unsatisfactory. George Michael enjoyed his years with Wham!, but in his subsequent career he has tried to become a more 'mature' songwriter. He now tries to appeal to 25-year-old men rather than 14-year-old girls; his fear, constantly expressed in interviews, is that he will be typecast as a teenybopper and not taken 'seriously'. This is not simply a plea from the heart of a creative artist who wishes his real message to be accepted after years of frivolity. He is too old to continue as a pop star for teenage girls. To be accepted by the young men who are the dominant album-buying group, he has to be portrayed as serious, as other than the girls' pin-up. Men are unlikely to admit to liking the artists adored, or previously adored, by their younger sisters, and will certainly not buy their albums. Yet the approval of men will be crucial if Michael is to continue to succeed in popular music.

As Michael's case so clearly shows, music is never made in a vacuum; it is always made within a set of cultural and economic imperatives, and for an identified audience. In Western culture, it is an audience with economic as well as cultural power, an audience with real power over the making of music. And yet the centre of power remains the actual process of making music, inside the studio. To this process we now turn.

Pop star or artist? Human League singer.

4 Inside the studio: producing music

'The studio' is one of the most powerful centres of the music business. Almost all the music we encounter casually on radio or television, in wine bar or supermarket, has been made in a recording studio. It is the centre of much investment and development. The mixing desk, with its rows of faders, appears on many album covers, signalling to us that the artists and producers involved are in command of this expensive and complex technology. Their power over this equipment is also power over us, the consumers of the music. Yet as we saw in chapter three their access to this power is itself the product of a much older power relationship, the contract. This chapter will look at relationships within the recording studio, and will also examine another area of the legal structure of the music industry, copyright law.

The connection between copyright and the studio is clear. The enormous sums of money earned through copyright agreements has been reinvested in the studios which are arguably over-capitalized. (In other words, so much money has been invested in the studios that huge profits are needed to repay the investment. This means that access to the recording and distribution process is increasingly restricted to a few, potential million-selling, projects). Increasingly, the record industry is becoming a constituent part of moves towards an integrated leisure system which *may* see the end of music-making as we now know it. But perhaps not: developments in studio technology offer many different routes into the musical future, and I will suggest some of these at the end of the chapter.

It is unarguable that the developing complexity of performance and recording technology has fundamentally changed power relationships within the structure of the music business. Since the mid-1960s the hegemony of the performer on stage and especially in the studio has been challenged by the pace and direction of innovation in music technology. In some forms of music-making, the performer as we know him or her has become simply outmoded: no longer necessary. Much of the chart music of today is made by people who would 20 years ago have been called producers rather than musicians. S'Express, Bomb the Bass and Jive Bunny, whose music is based on the sampler and the sequencer, are very different from the typical band of the 1960s, with three guitars and drums. Not everyone is happy about these changes. The writer Simon Frith has publicly lamented the 'death' of rock music as he knew it from the early 1960s onwards. While as we saw in the previous chapter

Is this really a band? The Beatmasters produce music without a guitar or drum kit in sight.

reports of this death are very much an exaggeration, (even the guitars and drums band is still going strong), there have been changes in the hierarchy of music-making, especially in the process of recording music. These changes have important positive and negative implications.

Before the 1960s the process of recording music was at the service of the songwriter or composer, and the performing musician. Up to this point, in fact, the history of recording is the story of continuing attempts to capture, as faithfully as possible, all the nuances of the musician's performance of a particular song or composition, as if the performer was giving a concert. In the early days this was a very difficult task. All recording was live and direct to the master disk which was used to press records. Recording was a single process, in other words. The performers played and sang for up to seven minutes (the limits of the 12-inch 78-rpm disk) and any mistakes could only be corrected by going through the whole process again. The acoustic recording technique, using a single microphone, made setting a balance between the various performers difficult. Usually the louder instruments and voices were placed further back in the room; occasionally, for the recording of popular songs, amplifying devices such as acoustic horns were added to violin bodies, and singers sang through megaphones. As this changed the sound even further away from the concert ideal, it was avoided wherever possible (especially for classical music).

In 1926 the invention of the electric microphone made things easier. Recording engineers developed multi-microphone techniques which allowed them much greater control over balance and allowed them to add artificial reverberation (which, paradoxically, was then intended to make instruments and voices sound more 'natural'). This gave recording engineers and record producers more control over the final sound, although their ideal was still to make recordings which were as close as possible to concert performance. Oddly enough, the recording process affected the way in which music was performed: jazz and popular songs tended to be written in four or seven minute units, so as to fit easily onto a single side of a record. Some jazz musicians still refer to a single recorded performance as a 'side'. Nevertheless, at this point the recording engineer and the producer were still basically at the service of the musician.

Three technical innovations increased the producer's control. The invention of magnetic recording tape in the 1940s finally ended the necessity to record complete performances direct to disk. Magnetic tape runs past a recording 'head' which makes a magnetic pattern on it. It is a much more flexible medium than disk recording. Tape can be re-recorded, and cut, and tapes of different performances or 'takes' can be spliced together. From then on the producer and engineer were able to splice together extracts from different performances on to a 'master tape' which in turn was used to cut the master disk which was used to press the records. Mistakes could be cut out through this editing process. However, the ideal was still the perfect performance, from the musicians' point of view. This ideal was at first underlined by the acceptance of stereo recording, and by the development of sophisticated 'hi-fi' record playing and radio broadcasting and receiving equipment, in the early 1960s. (Hi-fi stands for 'high fidelity', which means, again, as faithful as possible to the musicians' performance.)

The second innovation was the development of multi-track

recording, in the late 1950s and especially from the middle 1960s. Multi-track recording involves dividing the recording tape horizontally into separate sectors or 'tracks', each of which is addressed by a separate recording head. The tracks can be recorded or re-recorded simultaneously or individually. While musicians were still important (someone had to play all the material recorded), this development allowed the producer far more creativity. It was no longer necessary for all the performers to play at the same time. Individual musicians could record their voices or instruments on separate tracks, and they could also perform separately, on different days if convenient. More attention could be given to the individual components of the music: the sounds of the drums, the tuning of guitars or vocals, or mistakes by performers, could be corrected at leisure. Effects like reverberation and delay could be added to individual parts, again without the necessary presence of the musician. The whole process was controlled from the increasingly sophisticated console of the mixing desk, which allows the completely separate manipulation of individual tracks. Much more time was taken up in putting music together in this way than by everyone playing together simultaneously. The 'mix', in which the output from the multi-track tape recorder was passed through the mixing desk and recorded onto a separate master tape, was the final stage of the multi-track recording process. 'Mixing' in itself could now take as much time as the actual 'recording'.

These innovations in recording technique belonged mainly to the world of pop and rock music. Classical music continued to be made by the 'all play together' recording method, although there was increasing use in the 1970s of multi-channel balancing, which for the first time moved away from the concept of fidelity to concert sound and tried to 'improve' it by such means as boosting bass levels (e.g. on Decca records of the early-mid 1960s) and bringing wind instruments up in the mix for solo passages (as in many CBS and Deutsche Grammophon recordings of the early 1970s). But these were tentative steps, often frowned upon by record reviewers and the hi-fi purists: the late 1970s saw a return to 'direct to disc' recording, and to recording techniques in which a single pair of microphones was placed so as to simulate the ears of a single listener placed in the middle of a room – the return of the concert ideal.

Some version of the direct method of recording is almost always used for jazz, partly because it is cheaper than multi-tracking, and partly because jazz has its own strong tradition of great performers playing spontaneously. Pop and rock music had no such concert tradition to relate to: 'stadium rock', with its massive amplification, was developing in the late 1960s, *at the same time* as multi-channel stereo recording. Right from the start of rock'n'roll, a great deal of popular music was recorded according to the aesthetic values and technical possibilities of the studio, rather than the live performance (listen to the *deliberately* artificial-sounding echo-effect reverberation on Buddy Holly's 'Peggy Sue' and 'Rave On', for example).

It has often been noticed that albums, especially following the Beatles' *Sergeant Pepper's Lonely Hearts Club Band* (1967), became more expensive to make, as the multi-track recording process involved increasing amounts of studio time and increasing investment in recording technology. At the same time they were selling in larger quantities, displacing the seven-inch single as the most profitable record industry product. The sales potential of a band, and indeed of each album, would be carefully calculated by company accountants, and record companies became less likely to invest in projects other than potential million-sellers. It is said that WEA executives were in mourning for weeks after receiving the accountants' report on Fleetwood Mac's album *Tusk*, the follow-up to their hugely successful album *Rumours*. Even the WEA Christmas parties were cancelled! Sure enough, *Tusk* 'only' sold 8,000,000 units worldwide in its first year, as opposed to the 20,000,000 (plus four US no. 1 singles) clocked up by *Rumours*. Accountants are important to record companies: the implications of the advertisement reproduced here are worth thinking about.

So from the late 1960s albums were economically very important to record companies, who often invested very heavily in them in the expectation of enormous returns. Albums were also seen by music journalists writing in the late 1960s and early 1970s as setting the trend in the creative use of recording technology, and the 'album bands' the journalists liked so much certainly saw themselves as the most creative artists in popular music. But pop singles were also affected by these changes, and many pop producers were equally innovative and intelligent. Producer Phil Spector's 'wall of sound' singles of the early 1960s used monophonic multi-track technology to create a massive, almost oppressive sound. They were made by a small group of session musicians (including singers). The singles were released under the names of groups like the Ronettes and the Shangri-las (who only actually recorded them if they were conveniently available), and they were made to sound more like each other, *as singles*, than like the individual groups' sound. At least one Ronettes' single reached No.1 in the US charts without the group members even hearing it – they were on tour in Europe! Tamla Motown likewise had a 'house sound' based on the work of a few songwriters and session musicians. Singers, although they were the people with the star billing, had to fit in with the style; Marvin Gaye

The industry advertises for its most important employees.

complained that in the mid-1960s the Motown producers made him sing so high that his voice hurt. More recently, Madonna's voice is often made to sound higher and lighter (and therefore younger), especially for single releases, by the simple method of increasing the tape replay speed.

Fidelity to a notion of correct concert performance, and/or an attempt to show the artist at his or her best, are simply not in play here. The characteristic sound of individual studios, and the ability of the producer to manipulate the musicians' performances, rapidly became important considerations for record companies placing their

Casio keyboard demonstration. Shows like this at the music fairs may be the last chance to see that endangered species, the session musician.

artists for recording projects. In many cases the whole idea of making the same sort of music on record as live on stage was irrelevant. In the case of dub reggae in Jamaica, studio mixing techniques evolved in which, for long sections of tracks, groups of instruments would be cut out (to leave just bass and drums, for example). This developed initially without any reference to live performance. Few reggae bands actually play live in Jamaica, because of the costs of equipment. The Jamaican music scene focuses on the recording studio, with endless re-use of backing tracks played by a few session musicians, over which different singers sing different songs. The music is exposed to the public largely by DJs rather than live bands (indeed, the DJs are often the star performers). But reggae bands playing live in Britain quickly adopted the same dropout-mix dub sounds, and made them into performing techniques – another example of recording methods changing stage performance practice.

The third innovation which helped the 'rise of the producer' was the development in the 1970s of synthesizers, and in the 1980s of samplers and computer-based sequencing systems. This has confirmed the power of studio staff, but made the traditional musical performer virtually obsolete in many forms of popular music. The new power relations involved were quickly realized by musicians' unions, who have resisted both synthesizers and samplers with some ferocity, but without success. The position of 'pop stars' themselves is not under threat. Groups and solo singers are still necessary to promote records, even if they are merely good-looking figureheads who don't sing or play on those records, like Milli Vanilli (whose Grammy award was taken away in 1990 when their producers confessed that the stars hadn't sung a note on any of their singles). And as we saw in chapter three, many rock musicians and bands who *can* actually play and sing prefer not to use new technology, and continue to make successful music. The musicians most under threat from new technology are not bands but studio 'session musicians'. The people playing orchestral backing tracks (and often in the case of teenybop bands from the Monkees onwards, the rhythm tracks and lead vocals as well), are a threatened species. These are the union members, vital to the creation of popular music until the 1980s, whose future looks increasingly bleak. When in 1990 the *British Musicians' Union Journal* ran an advertisement for a sampler, the editor received hundreds of abusive letters from their own members, convinced that the sampler threatens their careers. Changing technology has taken their power and bestowed it elsewhere.

Microchip music technology has vastly increased the power of the production team – if they are computer literate. They can now manufacture the entire musical content of a track, including the vocals, as the court case involving the ZTT record company versus Frankie Goes to Hollywood indicated. Holly Johnson's voice was sampled a few times singing a few words, the rest of the band did little or nothing, and the magic fingers of producer Trevor Horn did the rest, producing seven remixed versions in all of 'Relax', the biggest single of 1984, with all seven featuring the massive drum sound which others have copied – usually by sampling the sound itself off CD. Similarly, Stock, Aitken and Waterman have recorded and produced a string of hits using very young performers, without employing session musicians or singers. The Pet Shop Boys can make very successful records, but they refused until recently to play live, on the grounds that they can't do on stage what they can in the studio. Bands like the Pet Shop Boys and more recent house music organizations like S'Express often consist of one singer and one computer programmer, and sometimes just a programmer who hires

Heaven 17, a successful early 1980s band who hardly ever performed outside the studio.

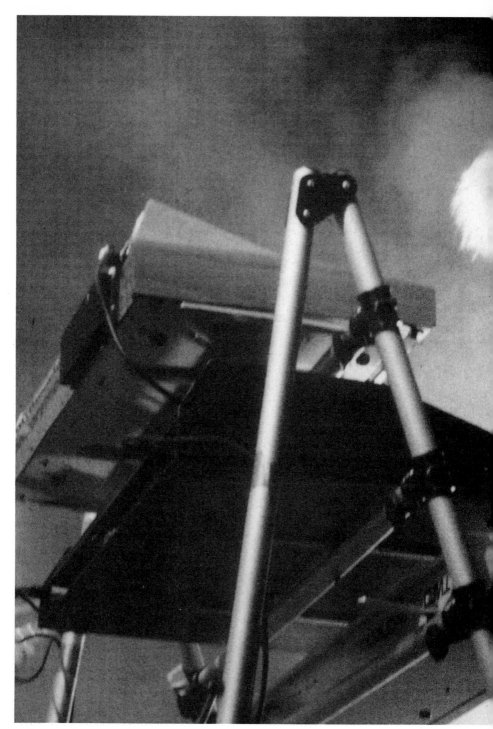

Anne Dudley of Art of Noise, a band which started as a couple of people in a studio but later went on to perform live on stage.

good-looking session singers or dancers to promote a record made entirely from sampled and synthesized sounds. They appear happily on stage with not a guitar or drum kit in sight. Musical power is now in the hands of the technologically aware, of the producer, sound engineer, mixer and remixer. Remixers like Jellybean, Dave Dorell and C J Mackintosh come to a project fresh, without playing any part in the recording of the multi-track, and remix it themselves either by manipulating what's there already, or by re-recording some or all of the backing tracks (hardly ever the lead vocals) to change the feel of the track. Issuing remixes, often at first through the clubs, is now part of the strategy to 'break' any single with a dance angle into the charts. Album buyers, too, are sometimes offered remixes: whole albums by Janet Jackson, Bobby Brown, Alexander O'Neal and Chaka Khan have been remixed and re-released, and the Madonna *Immaculate Collection* greatest hits album also consists entirely of remixes.

The implication of Simon Frith's lament over the end of rock music as he knows it is that all these changes in the hierarchy of music-making have been a Bad Thing. As it happens, there are several arguments to be made in their favour. The most important is that the advent of the sampler and sequencer has *liberated* music from the musician/performer. Musicianship up to this point was inherently elitist. It was also anti-democratic: opportunities for musical training in performance and composition are clearly restricted along class, ethnic and gender lines, and while the use of computer-based systems does require a form of literacy (which has to be learned), it does not require the years of dedication needed to produce the carefully-trained body virtuosity of the opera singer, the orchestral violinist, the jazz trumpeter, or the rock lead guitarist. The computer can enable people who cannot play instruments wonderfully well to create wonderful music.

You might think that virtuoso musicianship has always been irrelevant to pop music. Of course, not all popular music requires body virtuosity. Musicianship has often been less important in pop music than personality and energy. Punk in particular insisted that everyone could 'do it themselves', and this did something to undermine the notion of acceptable performance standards. However, punk was a short-lived phenomenon whose effects have always been vastly overrated by rock critics and sociologists who liked to look with approval for signs of teenage rebellion. It was the very competently played Fleetwood Mac album, *Rumours*, not *Never Mind the Bollocks* from the Sex Pistols, which dominated the American charts in 1977 – with the heavily orchestrated dance music of *Saturday Night Fever* not far behind.

As well as being closely related to wealth and opportunity, traditional musicianship is also elitist in the sense that body virtuosity – a type of athletic ability, in essence – is simply not distributed equally. Not everyone can be a great opera singer or jazz trumpeter, however much time they give to it. Sequencing software can do something to remedy this inequality, and help people, with a great deal of music in their heads but without the physical ability to acquire keyboard technique, to realize their ambitions. For many people, and especially for the physically disabled, this is a real advance. Many new kinds of music have been built around technological processes rather than playing or singing skills. A related point is that electro, hip-hop, scratching and house music have also displaced the singing voice (another skilled physical possession) and replaced it largely by 'rapping', rhythmic speech or chanting, over electronically created rhythm patterns. Toasting and ragamuffin in reggae are also styles which emphasize the speaking voice chanting over repeated patterns. These processes can be called democratic, opening up the ability to make music to many people who could otherwise be described as 'unmusical'.

There are also very negative ways of looking at these changes. Firstly the obvious (and equally valid) opposite position to the above: that technology without performance skills does devalue certain kinds of musicianship which give great pleasure to performer and audience alike. High technology pop music can be as bland, repetitive and unoriginal as any other form of music. There is the 'pre-set sounds' problem mentioned in chapter three. Much of the creative potential of the digital synthesizer systems of the last decade has remained unused. Routine patterns using routine synthesizer sounds abound in almost all popular music. Samplers, likewise, although capable of producing original sounds and layers of sounds through the manipulation and combination of samples, tend to be used merely to imitate. This is often boring. 1988 and 1989 heard a great deal too much of James Brown and his band via the sampler – especially of the 'funky drummer'. On the other hand, some of the musical collages of acid house mixes were genuinely original (and sometimes very funny). The sampling of well-known riffs and drum patterns also raises the most difficult issue associated with technological change: ownership and the vexed question of copyright law.

Copyright is the biggest and easiest earner in the music industry. The development of studio technology and techniques would not have happened without the enormous investment which record earnings has made possible: and these earnings are largely based on royalty payments. Every time a record is made, and every time a piece of music in copyright is performed in a licensed place or

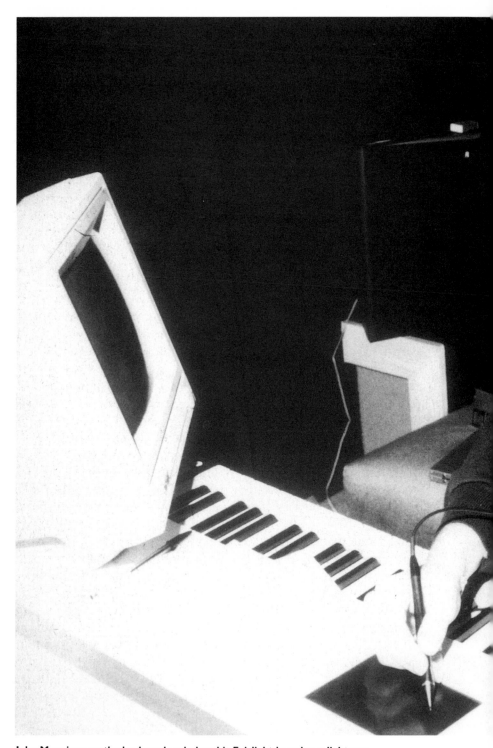

John Moss ignores the keyboard and plays his Fairlight by using a light pen.

broadcast by a licensed body, the owners of the copyright are entitled to a royalty payment. Collection agencies like PRS (the Performing Rights Society) and MCPS (the Mechanical Copyright Protection Society) function throughout the world by a series of reciprocal arrangements, and pour hundreds of millions of dollars every year into the coffers of music publishers and record companies. Multinational companies are therefore keen to buy other publishers' catalogues, which will earn them money for no effort. In 1988 Warner bought British music publisher Chappell outright. British electronics conglomerate Thorn EMI bought publisher SBK in early 1989 (and acquired the rights to 'Singin' in the Rain' among other titles) for £187 million, and went on to buy half of Charisma records (with classic rock acts such as Jethro Tull and more recent successes like Sinead O'Connor on their books) for £60 million.

Copyright is easy to deal with when ownership is settled and undisputed. In many cases it is not, and copyright in individual works is often tested in the courts. There are several problems: for instance, authorship and ownership are often unclear in the case of popular music from outside Europe and the USA. In 1989 a song called 'The Lambada' was a worldwide hit for the band Kaoma and their French producers, Olivier Lorsac and Jean Karakos. It was, the producers said, a Brazilian song whose original authors had been killed in a car crash. Hearing these claims, and the song, came as a surprise to two Bolivians, brothers Ulises and Gonzalo Hermosa, who claimed that the Kaoma 'Lambada' was in fact a version of a song of their own, 'Llorando se fue', which was in any case not a Brazilian *lambada* but a Bolivian *saya*. At the time of writing, the legal disputes around these questions had not been settled by the High Court in Paris. Even where authorship and first publication are not disputed, laws between countries are often different. In Denmark, copyright in sound recordings lasts for 20 years from the date of first publication. In the UK, it is 50 years. Although recent court cases have decided in favour of copyright holders, there are clear opportunities for companies to make copies of recordings out of copyright in one country, say Luxembourg, and sell them cheaply in another where the music is still in copyright, such as Germany. This then undercuts the copyright price, and the composer, performer and publishers lose out on their royalties. There are no current plans for harmonization in copyright law in Europe, despite moves towards a totally free market in the European Community.

Disputes over copyright are not a new problem for musicians and lawyers. Composers have often been accused of stealing other composer's musical ideas, and courts have decided whether this was so. Recent court cases of this kind involved George Harrison in 1974 over 'My Sweet Lord', and Vangelis in 1987 over the theme from the film *Chariots of Fire*. Now the appearance of the sampler has given a new edge to these disputes. Sampling often involves the taking and using of other people's riffs, drum patterns and sounds, and this has also involved litigation. In 1985 a remixer called Paul Hardcastle had a hit with a single called '19', an innovative anti-war song which used as its 'lyrics' or text sampled news reports from the Vietnam war. A great success for new technology, '19' was re-released in five remixed versions before it finally stopped selling. One of the patterns the song was constructed from was sampled from the early 1970s blockbuster album *Tubular Bells*, by Mike Oldfield. Virgin Records, owner of the copyright to *Tubular Bells*, claimed and won damages from Hardcastle. Virgin were awarded a royalty payment – a share of each record sold. Again, in early 1989 a throw-together band called M/A/R/R/S released a single called 'Pump Up the Volume'. This was also a big hit. Again, one of the patterns M/A/R/R/S used was taken from a song written and produced by Stock, Aitken and Waterman, 'Roadblock' – which was itself a pastiche of mid-1970s soul singles. Stock, Aitken and Waterman were also successful when they sued for damages. New technology's ability to make and use endless exact copies has drastically changed attitudes within the music business. Copyright law was always very important: it is now crucial to the survival of the industry in its current, massively corporate and massively profitable, form.

The most important aspect of this debate has been the continuing restriction placed by the recording side of the business on the sale of DAT (Digital Audio Tape) recorders and tapes. The technology has been available in Japan since 1985, and in Britain since 1988. Yet it would be an exaggeration to say that DAT machines were widely available in Britain – for most of this time they were only stocked in professional and home recording equipment retailers, not ordinary domestic hi-fi shops. Similarly, DAT was advertized in trade magazines aimed at professional musicians and recording engineers, but not in record or hi-fi magazines or the newspaper colour supplements. Record companies refused to issue material recorded on DAT tape. Instead cassette recorders, and cassettes using the inherently noisy and unreliable tape technology of the 1960s, were still marketed to the domestic consumer as if there were no alternative. Even after the record industry and the hardware makers met in Athens and thrashed out an agreement on the marketing of DAT, the machines themselves were very slow to arrive in consumer stores. Yet the Athens agreement means that DAT recorders are now built with disabling circuits which mean they are unable to make multiple copies. This is an astonishing concession by Japanese hi-fi manufacturers, and perhaps marks their defeat in one battle of the war to digitize sound reproduction, the more so as the pause between the arrival of the technology and its successful marketing to the domestic consumer has given Philips time to perfect its own digital recording system, DCC, which is compatible with ordinary analogue compact cassettes. At the time of writing the first recorders to use this system were expected to enter the market in late 1992.

One of these formats for digital recording will undoubtedly establish itself as replacement for analogue cassettes, whatever the opposition of the recording companies. The battle over CDs was won; falling prices established the hardware despite the software producers' unwillingness to invest in the necessary production systems, and the same laggardly record companies are now making enormous profits from the sales of products in this format. Many companies have stopped issuing classical music on vinyl LP; the demise of the vinyl pop single is promised before the end of 1992. Meanwhile, complaining bitterly of hard times and home taping, the record companies have managed to persuade many governments to impose a levy on blank cassette tapes. They have refused until very recently to produce any material in DAT format. One consequence of the continuing dispute has been that MCA and Columbia are now owned by Japanese companies: the hardware and software industries are moving towards a new corporate domination of the marketplace. From now on, Japanese companies will be able at will to release software products to match their hardware innovations. The next music recording format to be developed, erasable CD or CD-E, will undoubtedly be marketed with the cooperation of at least the Japanese-owned record companies. The immediate problems of copyright may be sidestepped by this, but the implications of changing technology for the money-earning possibilities of copyright will remain a crucial part of the development of the music industry throughout the 1990s.

It may be in fact that the multinational entertainments companies will move away from the system which has enriched them throughout the century. The implications of the purchase of Chappell by Warners, and Charisma by Thorn EMI, are that the days of the independent music publisher are over. Sony's purchase of Columbia likewise signals the end of the independent 'major' recording company. The balance is shifting in other directions as well. Music video was used in the early 1980s as a promotion tool. In other words videos were supplied 'free' to television stations which broadcast them, and the producers gained royalties, but also exposure for the relevant singles and albums. As the copying of any form of pro-

Matsushita pays £3bn for MCA

From **Tim Jackson** in Tokyo
and **Larry Black** in New York 27/11/90

N THE biggest film takeover, Matsushita Electric Industrial Co, the Japanese consumer electronics giant, yesterday signed an agreement to buy MCA Inc, the US entertainment conglomerate, for $6.1bn (£3.1bn).

Matsushita's products include Panasonic, Quasar and Technics. Its empire spans subsidiaries including JVC, which last month announced a separate joint venture with MCA in the music sector.

Matsushita's purchase of MCA underlines a growing conviction among makers of entertainment equipment that they also need to focus on software.

The deal is the third large foreign purchase of a US studio in the past year. Last autumn, Sony Corporation raised a storm of protest when it bought Columbia Pictures for $5bn; a month ago, an Italian-controlled company bought MGM/UA Communications for $1.3bn.

Matsushita, a conservative Osaka firm with 200,000 employees and sales last year of $38bn, has grown since its birth in 1918 to dominate first the Japanese and then the world electronics market. It is now the biggest maker of video cassette recorders.

The conglomerate also makes telephones, robots and sophisticated home appliances including computer-controlled washing machines and vacuum cleaners.

Analysts say the MCA purchase is the company's biggest gamble. However, Akio Tanii, Matsushita's president, argues that makers of electronic machinery need to own music and film companies in order to make sure software is available for their new products.

The MCA purchase will give Matsushita a film library, including gems such as *Jaws, ET,* and the *Back to the Future* trilogy.

In New York, the market welcomed the deal, although analysts said the total price of $71 a share was well shy of some of the figures that had been bandied about in recent months. But given the tight US credit market and the absence of any other buyers, MCA received a very good price, they said.

Matsushita is raising the $6.8bn purchase price internally, they noted, avoiding recourse to either US financial markets or Japan's weakened banks.

In midday trading in New York, MCA shares were up 50 cents at $65.825.

The fact that the troubled American firm had approached its Japanese partner asking to be taken over was revealed in September, when the MCA share price stood at about $34.50.

Matsushita will not be buying a New Jersey television station that belongs to MCA, because US government rules forbid foreigners from taking control of it. It also plans to sell MCA's restaurants and lodgings in the Yosemite National Park in California. Although Matsushita and the Japanese government appear keenly sensitive to political opposition to the takeover, the fact that Sony's purchase of Columbia was allowed to stand makes its difficult for politicians to interfere.

With this deal, four of the seven leading Hollywood studios, representing 38 per cent of last year's box office, will be in foreign hands.

"At this point it would be very much a case of crying long after the horse has left the barn," according to Christopher Dixon, entertainment analyst with Kidder Peabody in New York.

Lew Wasserman, MCA's chairman, said that his Japanese counterparts were committed to maintaining the creative independence for MCA. There have been fears that Japanese buyers of American media will be tempted to suppress anti-Japanese work.

Mr Wasserman also said the structural integrity of the group would be maintained, and that it would continue to operate under its own name and to be run by its existing management. There was no mention from the Japanese side of any firm guarantees on any of these points.

Leisure on the finance pages: *The Independent,* 27 November 1990. A typical headline story of recent years confirms another incursion by Japanese hardware manufacturers into the leisure software industry.

gramme material becomes easier, the trend is for producing companies to *charge* television directly for videos, in the same way as any other independent programme producer would charge the broadcast company for use of a programme it had made. The same trend is already evident in radio broadcasting.

These developments have to be seen in conjunction with continuing attempts to create an interactive leisure, education and communications system in the home. This is partly to be achieved through an extension of existing domestic electronic hardware. Home computers already function in this way to an extent. Teletext facilities encourage the direct purchase of goods from the home. Cable television is already available with an electronic shopping facility. Interactive CD, or CD-I, promises yet more in the way of integrated information and direct consumption. Text, image and music will be available in high resolution 'interactive' form (the user will be able to question, reorder and perhaps reprogram the software material – adding his or her chosen images to a favourite soundtrack, for example). The pattern of consumption is to be moved towards the screen and away from stand-alone music. It is no coincidence that the careers of Madonna, Prince and even Michael Jackson have incorporated film, with spin-offs in broadcast, video, soundtrack album and the like. The new model for the entertainments industry to follow may well be our subterranean friends the Teenage Mutant Ninja Turtles, a screen-based phenomenon that sells videos, records, books, soap, and anything else you care to think of, including of course, pizzas. Integrated marketing systems using screen-based information as their starting point will cushion the industry against the impact of increasingly exact home copying systems. The future multi-million dollar investment won't be in music as such, but music as part of a wider whole: the nineteenth-century composer Richard Wagner's dream of the totally integrated work of art will become a twenty-first century commercial reality, with the stress very much on 'commercial'.

These developments will also affect the making of music in the recording studio. If the arrangements are to the music industry's liking, and copyright remains enforceable as at present, the industry will continue to fund very large-scale projects, although these will tend to be in areas such as film soundtracks, and video-supported Fleetwood Mac albums, in order to maximize royalty returns on these projects. If, on the other hand, international copyright breaks down, and profitability within the music software industry falls drastically, it will cease to exist in its present form. More entertainment companies will be absorbed by Japanese hardware companies and will move to the screen-based global marketing position described above. In any case the often-announced 'death of the single' will soon be reality: there is by mutual agreement no place in the global leisure industry for the technology of the 1950s, or for the continuing losses suffered by the release of recordings on vinyl.

If this trend continues, it will leave a glaring gap in the marketplace for music-only products. The problem with screen-based systems is that we can close our eyes. Music, and especially recorded music, has the great advantage that it can be consumed without total concentration. In-car stereo and the Walkman are highly popular products precisely because they can entertain and inform the mind through the ears while the eyes are occupied elsewhere. Meanwhile videodisc has failed; the video Watchman and CD-Video are doing badly. Prerecorded video tapes don't sell particularly well, while video libraries do a good trade. Most people don't want to see films dozens of times, although they are quite happy to listen to their favourite albums on a daily basis. The industry hasn't quite understood this, or that video recorders are popular principally because of time shifting (recording television programmes to view when we want to see them, not when the company chooses to broadcast them). Visual imagery will never succeed in taking over the entertainment market completely.

The exception to the throwaway video rule: Laurie Andersen, an artist who has consistently shown how exciting the integration of visuals with sound can be.

Meanwhile, continuing innovation in music technology means that the recording of music can be done relatively cheaply to a good standard. Home-based multi-track recording, using a range of devices from cheap four-track cassette machines to state of the art computer hard disk recording systems, has already made all but the most expensive recording studios obsolete. As with all microchip technologies, many sophisticated devices are now affordable by the majority of the working population in the West. In this scenario of continuing innovation and the continuing spread of computer-based equipment to the home, the making of recorded music as such, without either the paraphernalia of record company support or the constraining values of physical musicianship, will become a more normal human activity (in the highly capitalized countries of Europe, North America and the Pacific at least). Small labels will become more important, and several models for their success are discussed in chapter six. One possible future development is the release of digital information down telephone lines, via modem and onto computer hard disc or CD-E, without the costly bother of record companies manufacturing their own discs or tapes. Integration of text, image and sound could in this instance provide the equivalent of the album jacket and sleeve-notes. 'Small labels' working in this way could of course include young people selling their 'recordings' in data form from their own bedrooms. The digital exchange of musical information is already well under way in fact; in Britain, the Composers' Desktop project and the UK MIDI Association service already offer data exchange over the telephone, and at the time of writing at least one small company was offering 'albums' of digital musical information on computer disk. These developments, taken with the projected future of the entertainments industry, in turn may well threaten the future of the highly capitalized, dedicated music recording studio. With luck, the future for the making of music in studios will be small and independent.

5 Reproducing the circuit

We learn to make music, and we also learn to use it in different ways. We often work to music; wash up to it; worship through it; dance to it or just to listen to it. This chapter explores the ways in which we learn to reproduce these divisions. The power structures involved in any form of music-making are not, as they may seem to be, 'natural'. Therefore changes in the positions offered to and taken up by anyone interested in music are possible, and other possible ways of making and using music are easy to imagine. Many changes, both positive and negative, are indeed happening already. Perhaps most importantly in the case of popular music, now that pop and rock music has a history, it has a sense of its own development and the strengths and weaknesses of past performing, recording and listening practices. Future generations of performers may build on the strengths and avoid some of the weaknesses.

Perhaps the principal weakness in the current structuring of music education is that it is elitist and divisive, restricting opportunities to a chosen few. Classical musicians and professional composers are clearly an elite. Most concert pianists, for example, show their potential at a very early age. Like other young people who control their bodies better than the average, and who become sportsmen and women, they are pressured to train hard, and continue to keep in shape by practicing repeatedly when they become professional. They usually go to special schools, and follow highly specialized courses at colleges or conservatoires, and universities, where the physical side of their chosen profession will be emphasized at least as much as any intellectual course of study. The most important non-physical study is of the ability to read music written using the Western tradition of notation – five-line staves containing 'notes' depicting pitch and length, like those printed overleaf. Concert performers see themselves as the guardians of a great tradition, performers of a very special body of work. Many of them have nothing to do with contemporary music, and only perform a few pieces written in the nineteenth century. Not all who train to become concert performers manage to succeed. The international concert and festival circuit, agents and record deals await the successful; the rest get by on a mixture of local concert engagements, teaching and other freelance work.

Classical composers, similarly, train to become continuers of the 'great tradition' of European art-music. To graduate as composers

Western music notation – a symbolic system which needs careful study. (Extract from *Continental Drift* courtesy of Simon Limbrick.)

they follow long and rigorous courses of study which involve critical appreciation, and often mimicking, of the work of previous generations of composers. They have to learn to read and write musical notation. Unlike performers, they will also study contemporary techniques of composition, including the uses of new music technology. And yet very few of the people trained will succeed in making a full-time career out of writing concert music. Some double up as critics or teachers; many experience regular periods of unemployment between commissions. Others, despite ambitions to write music for concert performance, end up doing hack-work of various kinds, writing for television, radio, and the theatre. Most graduates in composition fail to establish any professional standing: there are a few truly professional composers, and there are many less eminent people who are still 'composers' in the sense that they are trained and qualified to compose.

So there is a category of very highly trained people who make this kind of music. That leaves the rest of us as either 'appreciators' of that music, or completely untouched by it. The appreciation of classical music again is not a 'natural' condition. Most people do not in fact 'appreciate' classical music. They are alienated from its cultural and class base (although less so in some communities where performance is more democratic, as for example in Italy and Germany where there remain many small, local opera houses which are seen as part of the whole community). Classical music is presented as the cultural property of the educated middle class. Concerts are only advertised in the 'quality' newspapers. Tickets are often very expensive. Then too, people are alienated by the 'seriousness' of these events. Attendance at a symphony concert makes huge demands on silent concentration. To sit for periods of up to two hours in semi-darkness and concentrate on instrumental music unrelieved by dialogue or any sort of humour make these events painful rituals for many people. Opera is also boring to many people, even if they come from the 'right' economic background. Sponsorship suites and expensive stalls seats at the opera are often full of businessmen sleeping off the day's labours.

So listening to this kind of music is not natural, whatever the class position of the listener; it needs 'training' almost as much as performing the music needs training. This is often provided at an informal level. Radio announcers and programme-note writers inform the audience about the biographies of composers and their 'greatness', about the great tradition (the sequence of individual composers and stylistic schools), and provide narratives which help the listener along the music's lines of progression and development – like the music historians mentioned in chapter two. Another focus of informal training is provided by peer-groups, especially by hi-fi subcultures, people whose hobby is expensive sound-reproducing equipment. Such subcultures operate within many fields of middle-class life, such as schools and workplaces. Until the late 1960s, the best classical recordings made the best hi-fi demonstration records. The complexity of orchestral music, especially the wide contrasts in dynamics, display any turntable, amplifier and set of loudspeakers to advantage. Decca's recording of Wagner's opera *Das Rheingold*, released in 1957, entered the American popular album charts. This was principally because it was a superb technical achievement, an early justification of the new 'realism' of stereophonic recording, with its added sound effects like thunderclaps challenging even the best hi-fi systems of the time. Almost as a by-product, it proved that opera on record could be profitable. The success of *Das Rheingold* also confirmed Decca's plans to record the whole of Wagner's *Ring* cycle, and many other operas. The 'demonstration effect' continues to help classical music sales. Early CD players were also demonstrated with impressive classical recordings, notably the 1981 disc in which the Berlin Philharmonic Orchestra under Herbert von Karajan play Holst's *Planets*. CD is one factor in the current worldwide boom in sales of classical music recordings.

Formal training in 'music appreciation' is also available. Evening classes and school courses teach people how to enjoy *listening* to complex musical structures, in much the same way as courses in 'English Literature' at British universities teach not how to *write* but how to *read*. Music appreciation classes do not usually teach how to read music notation. The emphasis is again on the life and work of the individual composer, on the school of work with which they are associated, and on ways in which to respond to their productions, and the traditions of which they are a part. In performance, composition, and appreciation, classical music reproduces itself by emphasizing its history.

Traditionally, popular music has reproduced itself at almost every level by more informal means. Appreciation is firstly via radio and television, then by music papers, magazines, and ordinary newspapers. Tastes are further structured within record-collecting and tape-swapping peer-groups and dancing and clubbing subcultures formed from school and neighbourhood. Bands come from the same cultural jumping-off points. They are started in attics, bedrooms or garages, as young people try to learn riffs and vocal styles picked up from gigs or from other people's records. Early gigs are an important part of the learning process. If they go badly, it's usually curtains for the band. If they go well, then it's on to the stage of making demo tapes, finding agents, and pursuing the record deal. This informal training has so far managed to produce several generations of eager and often talented popular musicians. For most types of pop music, the extremes of skill required from the concert musician are not necessary – although there are still would-be guitar heroes who spend most of their time practising. Pop music doesn't demand the ability to read music notation. So while there are many successful pop musicians who *have* been trained in music at school or college (like Annie Lennox and Dave Stewart of Eurythmics), many more are informally trained.

Similarly, there is no accepted formal procedure, and no recognized qualification for the training of sound engineers. Traditionally in Britain there were two ways to train as a sound engineer. One way is for anyone wishing to work in a recording studio to write to as many studios as he or she can find addresses for, and simply beg for work. The lucky ones are taken on as 'tape-operators'. They load tapes onto reels, and make the tea, and watch and hopefully learn while others manipulate the recording equipment. This is no sort of apprenticeship, just a ludicrously unstructured, informal and exploitive training scheme, with no way for the trainee to assess his or her progress. Many 'tape-ops', fail to gain enough experience to then launch their own careers. In Britain until recently only the BBC had formally trained sound engineers – this is the second traditional route into studio work. All other employers of sound engineers either follow the hit-or-miss training procedure, or poach trained operators from the BBC or from each other. This may have been feasible when 1960s technology was being used, but is clearly an unsatisfactory state of affairs when complex computer-based systems are in constant use in all recording studios. Until very recently the only professional training in studio work outside the BBC was provided by private enterprise short courses, which provided no recognized qualification. Students on such courses often learn the hard way that qualifications which are not accepted by the relevant industry do not lead to jobs. And yet the problem of under-trained staff increases with every release of a new piece of studio technology. One hire company sent a 'trained operator' with every Fairlight CMI it hired out; when acquaintances of mine hired one, it turned out that even the trained operator could only work one relatively simple part of the operating system.

Not before time, this situation is changing. In the same way that classical music has a history, and is constantly aware of its tradition and trying to reproduce it, so also now is popular music. As we saw in chapter two, the new 'mature' popular music is now the subject of critical academic study. It is also the site of formal training. Since the late 1960s the study of the techniques of performance and composition in popular music have been increasingly available in music colleges, conservatoires and universities, and more recently in schools. The recent introduction of the GCSE music syllabus in England and Wales has meant that for the first time school students who are interested in pop music rather than classical music can complete a formal course of study including instrumental performance, recording and composition. They can compose using high technology instruments and four-track cassette recorders, for example. This questions the accepted notion of formal musical literacy. Using a drum machine, an electronic keyboard and a multi-track tape recorder anyone can make music which does not rely on the notation which is at the basis of Western musical training. Music which has not been 'written' and is not 'readable' in the accepted way can now be taught and assessed: rewarded within the academic framework, in other words.

For many people who feel alienated from the social and musical structures of classical music, this opening of the syllabus could be a very liberating experience. But what does this change mean in the context of cultural and commercial power relationships? It *could* indeed mean that at long last educationalists have woken up to the

The **TR727** drum machine and the Roland **MC500** microcomposer, two high technology instruments already used effectively by British school students.

fact that popular music also has aesthetic value, and that young people are capable of genuinely creative work in the medium. The new syllabus offers a real freedom. Young people can be allowed to compose, rather than to appreciate the compositions of others. At last their music and its associated values are being taken seriously by the education system. Yet this is a partial view of a complex change which has been driven by commercial rather than artistic pressures. It would be a serious misreading of this change in the educational syllabus to see it as supported by liberating and egalitarian ideas of aesthetic equality, something which sees the cultural place of

An example schoolchildren can follow: Erasure with their UMI-B, a composing system based on the educational BBC microcomputer.

popular musics as equivalent to classical music, and therefore a suitable object of formal study.

No doubt some educationalists have persuaded themselves that they are involved in such a liberating change. These kinds of changes in national aesthetic and educational values can undeniably take place. Certainly this was the case in America in the 1960s, for instance. One of the first fruits of the Civil Rights movement, as we saw in chapter two, was the social validation of jazz as both a 'great music', and the cultural property of the black American people. This validation was followed by the appearance of Black Studies courses on campuses all over the country, and many black music performers and composers – people like the jazz musician Donald Byrd – became professors of music, the exact professional equivalents of any other professor of music. This change then led to the academic study of many other non-classical musics.

The case of popular music studies in Britain is rather different. It does not mark an aesthetic or political recognition but principally an economic one. There are two ways in which government advisors and educational theorists see the changes in music education as important. In general, any subject in which children are genuinely interested, and which will involve them in learning to use new technology, is seen as a godsend in Britain. Britain, and more especially England and Wales, is the most educationally backward country in western Europe. Proportionately fewer people stay in education after the age of 16; fewer people complete technical apprenticeships; and fewer enter higher education, than in any other European country. This means that desperately-needed employment skills are absent in the workforce. Studying popular music is one of the ways in which young people can be trained to use the microcomputer-based equipment on which Britain's future economic prosperity depends. In particular, over and above its role in the training of people in general new technology skills, popular music is seen to be one of the most important individual contributors to the British economy. The pressure group representing the British recording industry, the BPI, constantly stresses the success of its products as exports in an economy with a balance of payments deficit. Many successful pop groups and solo artists *are* British, of course, but also important is the investment continually being made in recording studios, the availability of competent session musicians and recording engineers, and the importance of London as a centre for the music software business (music publishers and record labels). A great deal of music is made in Britain – and a great deal of money is made from this music. None of these positions of world power can be taken for granted. The appearance of new musical technology, almost all of it developed outside Britain, and the continuing lack of training provision, has led to the realization that structured training in the use of this equipment will be necessary in order to maintain the dominance of Britain in the production of certain kinds of popular music. The music industry has lobbied hard for the inclusion of music technology skills in school music courses.

This is not to say that commercial attitudes to music-making will necessarily prevail in British education in the 1990s. A furious debate took place in 1991 and 1992, after a Government-appointed committee had investigated the place of music in the school curriculum. Among the education advisers, music administrators and civil servants on the committee was just one professional composer, Mike Batt. A group of university-educated composers wrote to the papers, complaining that Batt is a composer of popular music for television, and even for children, and not a 'serious' composer like themselves, used to accepting state handouts in order to produce products of interest to a small minority. A few months later the committee produced a report which stressed that opportunities should be given to children to pursue interests in all kinds of music, and which gave examples of the kinds of music to be used to teach children about the basics of music: mentioning reggae, West African drumming and Indian ragas alongside European musical concepts like serialism, orchestration and score reading. There was an explosion of anger from another group who published letters and articles in the right-wing press, outraged that children might no longer be taught to venerate only music written by dead Europeans, and not at all interested in either cultural or economic reasons for giving children creative musical skills of their own. They insisted that European classical music was self-evidently better than music from other cultures, or popular European and American music. A powerful lobby group was formed to promote the case for 'traditional' music education. While the commercial pressures against it are formidable, it seems possible at the time of writing that school music may move back in the traditional direction.

Possible, but unlikely. Since contemporary classical music is as technology-based as pop music, almost all young musicians will need to use computers, samplers and so on. In the last decade courses in music technology have become available in many universities and music colleges, in Britain as elsewhere in the world. As yet such courses are restricted to the well-qualified few: predominantly, these are white middle class men, some of whom have gone on to work successfully in pop. But the industry is concerned that not enough people are coming through; what it needs is a larger supply of young people with experience of music technology, young people to perform and write, as well as record, the popular music of the future. To this end the industry decided not to wait for the outcome of negotiations over the place of music in the National Curriculum. The British Record Industry Trust, or BRIT, has been among the chief lobbyists for the setting up of new training courses

THE BRIT SCHOOL FOR
PERFORMING ARTS AND TECHNOLOGY

APPLY NOW

▶OPENING SEPTEMBER 1990◀

▶A P P L Y   N O W◀

The BRIT School
is a non fee-paying school with a difference.

You will be
leaving us not with just qualifications, but with
plenty of practical experiences, which have to do
with the world of the entertainment industry.

This is not just
performing, but also all of those vital technical jobs
which make up the industry.

If you are
either **13** or **16** on the 1st of September 1990,
ring us on 01-665 5446 for an application form.

Or write to
The BRIT School, P.O. Box 218, Croydon CR9 2XE.

Don't delay.
The closing date is 15th December 1989.

BRITISH
RECORD
INDUSTRY
TRUST

The BRIT School for Performing Arts and
Technology is a City College for the Technology
of the Arts, supported by the British Record
Industry Trust and the Department of
Education and Science.

An advertisement for the music industry's pet educational project, the **BRIT** school.

in popular music. The BRIT Trust has begun to set up a 'City Technology College' of its own in Croydon, a suburb of South London, with the blessing of the government. A rock concert staged at Knebworth in July 1990, broadcast on television and later marketed in album and video formats, provided some of the funding for this project. This college, which will select and train 12–16 year olds in music and technology skills, could provide future musicians and recording engineers, as well as more and better-qualified students for the similar courses already running at higher education institutions such as City University, Goldsmiths College, and the Universities of Surrey and York. The emphasis at the CTC will be slightly different, however. The orientation in Croydon will be towards popular music. In the higher education institutions people primarily training to be 'classical' composers are offered courses and facilities in music technology, electronic and electroacoustic music – again partly for purely commercial reasons. The use of electronics will help any would-be professional composer interested in writing for film, radio and television. The thinking behind the impetus to produce the next generation of technologically literate musicians is clear. They are not to become Great Artists, but competent artisans, and competent business people.

To emphasize this point, the City Technology College course, like the courses currently on offer in higher education, all include relevant aspects of business studies and legal studies. Future generations of pop musicians are less likely to be exploited by the agents and managers who took Elton John, Wham! and many others to the cleaners. Almost all young musicians will now know what a contract looks like, and how and where to get independent legal advice. The next generation of popular musicians will be legally as well as technologically literate.

One further sign of the increasing recognition of technical competence as part of the network of commercial advance is that music technology companies are themselves becoming increasingly active in education. Producers of music software like Steinberg and C-Lab offer cheaper educational versions of their popular sequencing programs, and they and many other companies also offer dedicated programs which help the child or student to explore interactively the possibilities in computerized music-making. Companies like Casio offer huge discounts for schools interested in their products.

One of the more remarkable corporate ventures into the field of education is by Yamaha. The Yamaha Music Foundation is a 'non-profit making' organization which in its own words is 'dedicated to helping children discover the everlasting joys of a life filled with music.' It publishes song books and music textbooks for every level of school music-making, and provides instruments, teachers and classes worldwide. It sponsors competitions, concerts and recordings. All over the world, Yamaha employs educationalists and teachers to take the high-technology gospel into the classroom. The commercial spin-off from this kind of organization is clear: someone who has been exposed to music via Yamaha instruments, amplifiers and so on will be likely to continue using them when he or she becomes an adult, whether musician, consumer of hi-fi, or parent of the next generation of Yamaha-using children. The power circuit often involves generating permanent feedback; here is a clear example. (Although this should not be written off as pure cynicism or pure exploitation in the same way as cigarette-dumping in the 'Third World': Yamaha orchestral and band instruments, like their high technology instruments, pianos and other musical equipment, are almost always well-designed, reliable and pleasurable to use. They did not pay me for saying this).

In the medium-term future we should see far more young musicians educated to a higher technical standard and aware of the commercial as well as the creative aspects of the music business. So that's alright then. Or is it? There are several immediate problems with this new appearance of popular music in education. The first became clear during the emergence of black popular music as a higher education subject in America in the 1960s. Studying a body of techniques under formal tuition is for most people a brake on creativity. Classical composers or musicians have been trained on these principles for generations. They accept that only the very few 'greatest' individuals have anything worth saying, and indeed very few individual voices emerge from this uniforming process. The rest 'fail'; they either become hack composers, or teachers, or they leave the profession of music altogether. Most professional composers produce work which copies or takes from accepted styles, without adding significantly to those styles.

The same limits on creativity and originality apply to the formal study of popular music. While jazz, for example, is also an elitist practice, the development of the music was not formally structured into a 'tradition'. Jazz depended above all on the combination of composition and improvisation as the expressions of the individual artist. The danger is that the learning of jazz saxophone or guitar *as an accepted body of styles and techniques* tends to make sax or guitar players who sound like previous generations of sax or guitar players, and also to make further generations of teachers who teach only those stylistic skills. Many high school or university graduates in jazz who have emerged since the 1960s – such as the (white) American saxophonist Scott Hamilton – play, quite deliberately, in

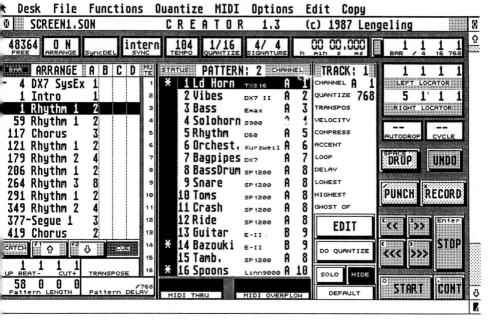

The C-Lab sequencing program; the manufacturers offer a discount to educational establishments, hoping that students who use it will eventually buy their own copies.

The Yamaha foundation will no doubt increase the use of Yamaha instruments as a by-product of its educational work.

the style of a previous generation. Jazz creativity is denied, however much the product sounds 'genuine'. It is no coincidence that in the 1960s, at the precise point at which the academic study of jazz history emerged, the history of jazz slowed down; jazz performances by bands considered to be in the forefront of the music's development, such as the Art Ensemble of Chicago and the World Saxophone Quartet, became recyclings of jazz history. Similarly, the young players associated with the British 'jazz revival' of the late 1980s were almost all competent players of 'hard bop', a style of the 1950s which emphasizes body virtuosity. And nothing else.

Pop music performance and songwriting are less inherently elitist. With one or two exceptions (for example, heavy metal, the older generation 'pomp-rock' of bands like Pink Floyd and Genesis, and the recent guitar bands of the Manchester 1960s revival) very little depends on body virtuosity attained by years of dedicated practice. Even in the field of electronic dance music and hip-hop, the emphasis is on the simple and catchy. Formal tuition will still tend to the recycling of sameness, in the ways outlined above. Learning how to do it at school (which often means learning to please teacher, learning to pass) will brake creativity and experiment. We need informal networks and peer groups without official sanction or supervision to keep evolving and developing their own codes of musical use and pleasure: even in the age of the sampler, originality and humour are possible.

I suspect that originality in popular music will always owe more to the informal academies of the bedroom, the garage, and the small club, which are also democratic in a way no formal study can be. In particular, failure is democratic. Informal music-making lets everyone participate, and often agree that they aren't up to it, can't sing in tune or play in time. The study of music at school is always elitist, involving notions of success and failure imposed from outside the peer-group. If popular music does become academicized, and the boy or girl next door does not choose to take music at school, then this will reinforce the existing divisions between the practices of making and consuming music. One obvious point is that of the alienation of girls from music-making. Young women are often denied access to instruments, and prevented from joining bands, from within their own youth cultures: they are seen as users of music (as attenders of certain types of gigs, as readers of certain types of music papers, and as dancers) rather than as musicians or even potential musicians in their own right. It could be argued that this will be less likely to happen at school, where teachers can encourage the breakdown of this conservative and male-dominated musical culture. However, music is increasingly going to be taught as a branch of technology, and this is precisely the area of formal education from which women feel most excluded. This process is accentuated rather than diminished at school, where efforts by teachers have so far failed: girls tend to choose humanities rather than scientific and technical subjects. Courses based on high technology will have to make great efforts to include women, or the existing patterns of gender employment within the music business will simply be reinforced. The BRIT college will use its power to reproduce its existing power structures. The artificial division of the world between the musicians and the rest, including this gender division, will be strengthened through the system of selection and qualification.

If music-making outside the classroom does not survive, then we will be left as 'appreciators', as fans, and we will have less control over the shape and direction of music. In view of the developments discussed in chapter four, this would be a danger indeed. In conclusion, however, we will see that there are ways in which new musics can evolve outside the formal structures of classroom and industry.

6 Conclusion
The renewal of music?

This has been a book informed by theory, rather than a text which presents and debates theoretical issues as if they were as interesting or important as the business of musical production and consumption. But if we are to attempt to sum up the condition of music in the present, and to discuss possible musical futures, one theoretical debate needs a more specific mention. We live, we are often told, in a 'postmodern' age, in which all the certainties of aesthetic values and pleasures have been abandoned. There remain healthy debates about the status of the term 'postmodernism' – critics of the term see it as a form of disengagement with any kind of progressive politics, while its supporters argue that it is the only comprehensible way of seeing current realities. It is unarguably a genuine theoretical approach, and since it deals with the changes in the global economy which continue to affect the music business, we should at least approach some of its arguments.

The postmodern economy has seen the reorganization of capital across a few world centres. New York, Tokyo, and London are now held together in a twenty-four hour abundance of information which serves the ends of a few very large transnational companies. This defiance of day, night and the seasons threatens all other certainties of time and space, including the nation state, and including even history as we have known it. When the empire of the Soviet Union was falling apart in late 1989, the American commentator Francis Fukuyama proclaimed the 'death of history' and the final victory of unfettered global capitalism. Certainly one way to interpret the recent history of the music business reinforces the viewpoint. Fredric Dannen's recent book *The Hit Men* tells the story of the major American record companies – a story highlighting greed, corruption and organized crime, played out by men with little or no love for music. The final section of the book tells of the buying of CBS/Columbia by Sony, and the emergence of a global giant intent on integrating the whole of music economics – software (writing, recording, publishing, film and video) plus hardware (hi-fi, television, video recorders and so on) – into one system. Sony was able to mount the takeover partly because of CBS's poor profitability, which was due to the company's conservatism and its continuing reliance on old rock and r'n'b acts. One implication is that the transnational companies like Sony and Polygram will simply inherit this conservatism, and will now use their power to market the huge publishing catalogues they have acquired, attempting to provide uniform cultural products across existing political boundaries, via satellite television as well as more traditional media.

This prospect raises genuine fears for the survival of independent cultures, including independent musical cultures. Such fears have been voiced before. The impact of the cassette was ambivalent, as it provided opportunities for local music as well as flooding the world with Anglo-American pop. The impact of an industry in which hardware and software are provided by the same company, and in which the possibilities of using its media are limited by devices such as copycode, could be devastating. Critics of global capitalism argue that where aspects of national cultures survive, they will lose their uniqueness, and become part of one system. This will happen to popular musics as it has already happened to pizzas; foods which were once from different cultures are available all over the world in an undifferentiated supply. Similarly, music will continue to draw on many different styles: far from creating exciting new hybrid forms, the mix of styles will be homogenised into one transcultural style without political or aesthetic differences.

Dannen's book presents a gloomy picture, and a paranoid view of a boundaryless postmodern culture can deepen the gloom. But there are other ways to read the story: this final chapter discusses the recent past and potential future of the making of music, giving examples of developments which have both subverted and changed the music business. Even the perspective of the postmodern can be presented in an optimistic light. Neither new technologies or new developments in the role of capital can predetermine their own outcomes: it is certain that new national and ethnic identities, and new cultural practices (including new musics) will emerge, as they always have done. Rumours of the death of cultural history have been greatly exaggerated.

To return to the important question posed at the beginning of the book: in the end, we are all responsible for music; in which case, all is not lost. There is no need for popular music to disappear from history, and to be caught in the endless recycling of existing forms in a postmodern world without meaning. There is no need for the pleasures of classical music to be restricted to a self-proclaimed elite. Music can remain important to large numbers of people, who if they try hard enough can create successful musical movements. There are many ways in which music can live, despite the conservative wishes of the music business, and some are itemized here. There are examples of people choosing to try to work outside the constraints of the musical economy altogether, and illustrations of the transformation of the business itself.

Ignoring the business

Musics can and do flourish outside the formal structures of the music business. Music is part of any community, and local community groups and local political organizations often encourage music making: seen here is an advertisement for a recording studio run by a London borough for the use of local people. The studio is well equipped, and is available for hire cheaply. Basic courses in recording technologies and techniques are available. The potential here for a strong non-commercial tradition of music-making is slight, given the lack of resources currently available for local government; but it should be noted that the State's chief distributor of subsidy, the Arts Council, published a discussion document in early 1992 which opened up the possibility of direct government subsidy for rock music for the first time in Britain (some rock musics already receive subsidy elsewhere in Europe). As with the controversy over the place of music in the national curriculum, this document sparked angry debate: again, we should merely record that there is potential here for the development of musics without immediate pressure for commercial success.

Of course, there are already many ways of making music which exist quite happily outside the economic restraints of the music business. Amateur choirs, orchestras, bands, folk groups and so on are to be found virtually everywhere. Existing non-commercial traditions are provided by religious and political groups, which often maintain and develop musical styles of their own: music of the churches, the chants of the Buddhist and Hare Krishna movements, and for that matter the music of the heavily left-wing British 'folk revival' of the 1960s and after, are all dependent on particular meeting-based moments of celebration which only seldom cross over into the commercial world of recording. The less determinedly anti-capitalist musics of the counter-culture 'hippies' of the late 1960s emerged from a similar culture of celebration, but were quickly incorporated into the mainstream music business, despite the apparent attitudes of some of the performers. Punk, likewise, spat its way into the charts while affecting disdain for the values of an industry which had grown fat on the music of the previous generation.

But not all punk outfits chose to kiss the hands that paid them. One which remained as far outside the system as it could, Crass, was the outstanding punk band in many ways. The founder of Crass, Penny Rimbaud, was a typical British radical popular musician, educated at public school and art college. He brought some of the values of the hippy movement, its love of drugs and free

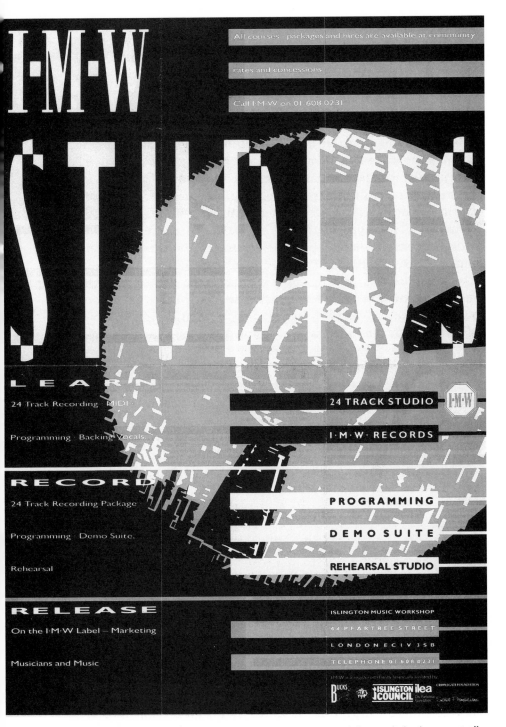

Islington Council's answer to the commercial pressures of the music business: a studio of their own.

festivals, and its contempt for the police, together with the anger and hatred of all establishment practices which was displayed by the punks. The band's songs focussed on the broad issues of the environment, nuclear power, and the British class system, as well as more specific issues such as the Falklands War. Crass preserved its integrity against what it saw as the corruption of record industry values by playing for several years on a gig circuit which was publicised entirely at street level, by word of mouth and by graffiti. The audience was in the main young and working class. An anarchist political movement, Class War, grew out of these gigs, and adopted the anarchist graffiti symbol used by Crass (an A in a circle) as its insignia. The gigs were held late at night in unusual venues like church halls and community centres, and they received very little coverage from the music press. Nevertheless, the band released several records, which sold well without any radio exposure – but they refused on principle to supply records to the shops which were sampled for the Top 40, so they never appeared in the charts, and never appeared on the *Top of the Pops* television show, the crowning moment for the career of many British bands. Crass split up in 1984, but Class War still uses their music as a rallying point for its ideas about the nature of the British state. Crass songs were well to the fore in the Class War celebrations which followed the riots in Trafalgar Square in March 1990. Crass, and the ideas as well as the music it generated, remains important to this (very small) British subculture. Similarly, on the extreme right of British politics, neo-Nazi bands like Skrewdriver thrash their way through gigs to the delight of their skinhead followers: like Crass, their gigs are for the faithful only, and are not generally advertised; here, perhaps, the music press ignores these events as a matter of principle.

Subverting the business

In America in the 1970s the Baby Boomer generation which had encountered rock'n'roll as teenagers (and grown through the sixties listening to rock and soul music) had reached thirtysomething. They faced a dilemma: were they too old for the popular music offered to them by the record companies? If not, no problem; but if so, what should they listen to? One option was to continue to listen to the Grateful Dead, James Brown or the Rolling Stones. Many did: and many artists of their generation continued (and continue) to perform and record for them. Another option was to start listening to classical music, opera, or jazz. Again, many did: the fortunes of all three forms have been improving through the 1980s. Yet another option was to remake music to suit their own tastes, using what they liked about existing forms. Once again, some did: a music evolved in and around California which was without the anger of jazz and r'n'b, the brashness of youth pop, or the snobbery of opera. This music tends to be quiet, and most of it is instrumental rather than vocal. Stylistically, much of it built on the success of 'minimalism' in the late 1960s: the music of classically-trained composers like Steve Reich, Philip Glass and Terry Riley. The minimalists had rebelled against the values of avant-garde 'classical' music (written by composers such as Webern, Nono, and Boulez, this music dealt with rhythm and harmony through complex mathematical processes; the result is difficult both to perform and to listen to). The minimalist rebels produced a music which stressed the repetition of simple harmonic structures which change very slowly. Other significant influences were the electric jazz of Miles Davis's groups of the late 1960s, notably the album *In A Silent Way*, and nineteenth and early twentieth century classical piano music, especially that of French composers such as Debussy and Erik Satie. This new style of music became popular in concerts and radio broadcasts, but at first mainstream record companies saw no commercial potential and would not bother with it.

So a group of people set up a record label of their own and started selling records from the back of a truck at concerts of 'their' music. The Windham Hill label went on in the 1980s to become a worldwide commercial success. The music business was wrong: there was nothing inherently uncommercial about quiet or repetitive music. Phillip Glass, one of the early minimalists, has become a hugely successful crossover musician, recording albums for CBS marketed under 'rock', and also writing several very popular operas. The music associated with Windham Hill, often called 'New Age', has quickly become an established category, with many dedicated radio stations in America, and has spawned many commercially successful imitators in Europe. Polygram's Theta label, and the Coda offshoot of the British label Beggar's Banquet, produce their own versions of New Age music (though it has to be said that their products sell better in America and mainland Europe than Great Britain, where someone once remarked that New Age music is 'music for people who don't like music'). One recent innovation in New Age programming is the Landscape Channel, in which instrumental music is combined with landscape images, and the pieces of music being played are offered for sale to satellite subscribers. Windham Hill meanwhile continues to be a success, and now has a Jazz offshoot (just to underline that its main label's music is not jazz). Windham Hill achieved success despite the record industry's conservatism, because it provided a popular product for a new type of audience.

Transforming the business

But we don't have to look to the affluent middle class of California, or the angry underclass of contemporary Britain, to find new ideas and new musical forms which have changed the ways in which music is produced and consumed. The Acid House movement in Britain provides an example of a new musical style which changed the way in which the music business worked – including the pop charts – as well as, again, providing a product for a new audience. The new audience was young and comparatively affluent, at its point of origin basking in the overheated economy of Thatcherite Britain; appropriately enough, a new hedonistic subculture emerged from people who had been basking in the heat of Ibiza. In the summer of 1988 young people in Britain began to form clubs in order to continue celebrating the holiday culture they enjoyed in Spanish resorts. The music in place here, at first known as 'Balearic Beat', blended elements of the rhythmic repetitions and banal lyrics of Eurodisco with the more experimental, but equally repetitive and synthesiser-based, 'house' music of Chicago gay clubs. British DJs were quick to adopt one of the more extreme forms of house music, 'acid house' – and during the summer of 1988 young people were so eager to dance to it that a flourishing culture of illegal warehouse parties or 'raves' grew all over the country. These parties became headline news in the press, partly because they were very big events, with attendances often reaching 20,000 and more; partly because they were associated with drugs, especially LSD ('Acid') and the more recent import, MDMA ('Ecstasy'). Several of these parties were raided by the police; eventually a back-bench member of parliament made a name for himself by passing an Act to increase

THE INDEPENDENT

MONDAY 23 JULY 1990   ★★★ Published in London 35p

Police arrest 836 in raid on Acid House party

By Stephen Ward

POLICE WITH riot gear, horses and dogs broke up a huge Acid House party on the outskirts of Leeds yesterday and detained 836 people in one of the biggest mass arrests in decades.

Under a tougher law which came into force 10 days ago, the organisers of unlicensed parties face up to six months in prison and a £20,000 fine.

Yesterday's party was being held, apparently without the owner's permission, in an empty warehouse in Gildersome, near a junction of the M62. When officers moved in at 5am they were met with a hail of bricks and pieces of furniture.

The warehouse was badly damaged and its windows smashed. Drugs worth more than £2,000, including LSD, cannabis and amphetamines, were found, police said.

All those arrested were held and questioned for several hours at 26 police stations as the police tried to find the ringleaders. Most of the partygoers were released late yesterday. Many complained

that the police had used excessive force to arrest them.

Young people from all over northern England had begun arriving by car at the warehouse at about 2am yesterday, paying £6 for entry. The police had a tip-off from a security guard near by, and stopped about 1,000 more people reaching the party.

West Yorkshire police issued a statement, to which it refused to add anything, saying: "A number of police officers were injured, three of whom required hospital treatment. One officer required stitches to a gash in the jaw after

being hit with a four-foot plank. Two others were taken to hospital with hand and wrist injuries."

Those who could be connected with the damage and with organising the event, and with drugs offences, would be appearing in court "in due course", the statement added. The police have to pass on names of organisers of unlicensed parties for the local authority to prosecute.

The new law, which came into force on 13 July, was introduced by Graham Bright, a Tory backbench MP, with government support. It gives magistrates summary powers

to pass the new penalties without having to refer cases to a Crown Court. Previously, the maximum sentence for an unlicensed party was £2,000 fine, in London only, three months in prison.

Mr Bright, who believes that drugs worth £30,000 to £90,000 can be sold at a single party, said: "I want to see magistrates dish it out as a signal to anyone thinking of organising an Acid House party. My main worry is safety. The conditions are unbelievable – you get several thousand people in a warehouse with no firefighting equipment and no

emergency exits. If there was a flash fire, as we saw at King's Cross, everybody would be roasted alive. Because the organisation is ad hoc, cars block the roads all around so the fire services could not reach the party if they were called."

He said Acid House parties were organised by leaving a recorded message on a mobile telephone number, ownership of which would be changed several times to make it virtually impossible to trace.

The message would give a rendezvous point, often a motorway

service station. There would often be two or three more rendezvous points before partygoers learn the final destination.

"It is all clandestine, but highly sophisticated, using CB radios and mobile phones," Mr Bright said. It was extremely unlikely that the backers would risk being at the party.

Police arrested 430 people during poll tax riots in the West End of London on 31 March this year. Another 70 were held later after police identified more people who they said were involved.

Police criticised, page 2

New forms of identity celebrated by some are feared by others: the *Independent* newspaper, 23 July 1990, reports police intervention to close down an illegal party.

penalties against the promoters of such parties, and police intervention against them continued. This amounted to a media-led 'moral panic' about the subculture, as with virtually every other new collective allegiance celebrated by young people since the 1950s. Meanwhile, the music itself was taken up by the more orthodox club scene; and it made a big impact in the charts. And it transformned the ways in which the charts were constituted.

The music of the Acid House summer was notable, if not unique in British pop music, because of its almost total reliance on computer-based technology: the sequencer, the sampler, and the synthesiser (and especially the older analogue instruments like the Minimoog). And in two ways it transformed the way voices were heard. For the first time in British pop, the spoken voice, rap, became a commonplace. But in many of these tracks lyrics (whether spoken or sung) were less important than the all-important drum patterns and bass riffs. The voice, the crucial sound of virtually all Anglo-American popular music since the brief heyday of the big band in the 1940s, was relegated from its leading position and used, cut and sampled just like any other instrument or sound: listen for example to Simon Harris's 'Bass (how low can you go?)' or more radically, Bomb the Bass's 'Beat Dis'. Furthermore, this music was made cheaply, often in small home-based studios, by young people like Bomb the Bass's Tim Simenon. This both undermined notions of the 'band' (while not of course simply replacing it) and helped to challenge the importance of the highly-paid and often very conservative record producer. The success of this music, whether produced in a full studio or the artist's bedroom, finally signalled the importance of dance music built with affordable technology: at the time of writing dance tracks made using these techniques continue to dominate the pop charts. While we should remember that the formula dance pop of Stock, Aitken and Waterman was also very successful in these years, the success of acid house and its many derivatives has proved that the highly conservative music business can still be transformed by popular demand.

So music doesn't have to be what the major record companies which dominate the music business wants. People's needs for different forms of expression can be satisfied in all sorts of ways either inside or outside the dominant power structures of music. Crass subverted them, and were successful for a while, on their own terms; and in the case of the Windham Hill label and the acid house phenomenon, they actually changed those power structures. Other movements and organizations can also work to subvert or transform existing musical practices. Women in Music is now an established organization which operates a catalogue of recordings written,

Simon Harris tries to demonstrate how low his bass can go.

produced and performed by women, which again operates outside the 'major' labels and their distribution schemes. In late 1990 a successful two-month festival of musics written and performed by women was held in London. It offered a challenge not just to the male-dominated music business, but also, through the range of its activities, the established categories such as jazz, classical music, and folk music. The World Music phenomenon has also changed the way the music business works. The annual WOMAD (world festival of music and dance) which started as a small free festival, is now one of the most important events of the British musical year. The mid-1980s success of some African pop musics has made international stars of performers like Salif Keita. The private release of the *Mysteres des voix Bulgares* album, which was almost immediately bought up by a major label, has been followed by two more albums, and tours by Bulgarian singers. Certainly there is an element of fashion in all this – African pop was less popular in Britain in 1992 than 1987; for a while in the middle 1980s it was impossible to attend a middle class dinner party without hearing Bulgarian voices issuing from the hifi. There is also an element of postmodern 'pick and mix' at work here – with the musics abstracted from their cultures, and the usual unequal power relationships (described here in chapter two) operating against the producers of the music. But in the interim all these musics have become part of general Western musical consciousness. This has led to changes in public taste, despite the conservative resistance of the 'majors'.

Re-using music

There is, then, comparatively little danger that a single, universal culture will simply be imposed by the transnational leisure industry. Far from it. A single musical style simply cannot encompass the many ways in which music is used within any single culture, let alone this still very multicultural world as a whole. In the examples above, a music or musical practice is a crucial part of the formation of a particular identity: and identities are constantly being reworked and reasserted through music. Women in Music emphasizes the centrality of gender as the instrument of opportunity for musical performance; classical conductor Jane Glover and jazz pianist Laka Daisical can unite in this aspect of their musicality, despite their different musical practices. Crass and Skrewdriver are central to the formation of very different political identities among people from similar class backgrounds. Both 'New Age' music and the musics of the 'rave' culture are important to the formation of specific identities based on age rather than class, politics, ethnicity, gender or sexuality.

Tim Simenon poses in front of his Minimoog, a typical Acid House instrument.

Clubs dealing in other musics – Bhangra all-day clubs, soul week-enders, and gay discos – can all offer similar whole or fragmentary identities to those who use them.

One very important reworking of identities as the world moves into the 1990s concerns nationality. The disintegration of the Soviet empire and the gradual moves towards Western European unity have both, paradoxically, served to highlight the increasing import-ance of the locality and the small state as opposed to the nation-state of the late nineteenth century. The long and painful death of Yugoslavia, gradually reverting to its component parts, and the fragmenting of the old Soviet Union into a very loose federal struc-ture, emphasize this re-emergence of the locality as the base for a new politics of ethnic identity. Here, as elsewhere, music continues to play an important part. This is not necessarily politically wel-comed. Throughout Europe the revival of petty nationalism has been accompanied by equally petty racisms: Skrewdriver is far from being the only post-punk band which thrives on the 'patriotism' of anti-semitism and calls for the repatriation of immigrants. However, the emergence of local musics within Europe provides another reminder of the probability that the moment of global cultural uniformity will be deferred.

Many of these expressions of cultural nationalism can be seen more positively. Rock music and avant-garde jazz were important as a source of nationally-based opposition to the State within the East Europe of the Iron Curtain: so also was the work of some classical composers. One of the first acts of the new State of Georgia was to send its symphony orchestra on a European tour. The Georgian State Symphony included in its programme music by a Russian, Tchaikovsky; but also the work of a Georgian composer, Gia Kan-chelli, whose fifth symphony was broadcast in Britain for the first time. Music has also played a part in the continuing cultural frag-mentation of the British Isles. Irish, Welsh and Scottish bands have helped to maintain the Celtic languages, and to maintain the identity of those who feel threatened by the political uniformity of control from Westminster. The London-based band The Pogues have helped to promote a distinct Irish culture within the metropolitan city; bands like Runrig have been at the forefront of the movement for an independent Scotland; the Factory label in Manchester has reas-serted the cultural difference of the North-West of England; distinct musical cultures also flourish in the North-East and West of the country. Anglo-Caribbean musics are as differentiated by locality as white English pop: compare the work of the metropolitan Soul II Soul with the Bristol based Massive Attack. Throughout Europe, local musics of this sort are being recreated, and attract passionate

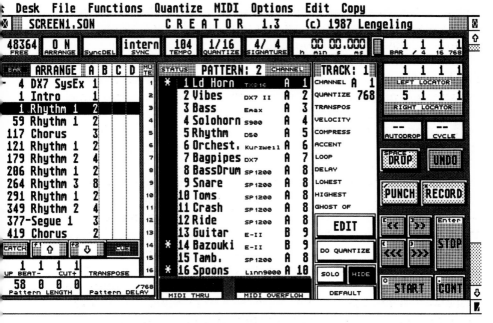

C-Lab's *Creator*, **a powerful program developed by a small independent company. Will such innovations continue?**

local support, whether or not they go on to become commercially successful. Local and ethnic identities are also supported in the United States, with neighbourhood-based rap acts in the cities reflecting different ethnic makeups (mixed black, Hispanic and white input) as distinctive as country musics outside them (mixing different blends of Irish, Scottish, German and other European sources, often also with black input).

Remaking music

Even without the powerful drives provided by the need for the construction and negotiation of new identities, musical innovation need not succumb to the totalizing aspirations of the leisure industry. It should be said, indeed, that the compressions of space and time implied by the development of the global economy have not yet ironed out cultural differences even within the leaders of the music business. Fredric Dannen's book highlights differences between Italian–American and Jewish–American practices. Continuing cultural differences among Americans, Japanese and Europeans are clearly signalled by their very different interpretations of economic signs. In many ways, in fact, global capitalism recognises the importance of catering for difference: 'niche marketing' practised from Japan assumes that Europeans have different aesthetics of hearing, and most Japanese firms provide specific sets of voices for synthesisers sold in various parts of the world. Similarly, many Japanese consumer electronics companies market loudspeakers with different tonal qualities in Europe and Asia: Sony have recently built on this principle and marketed a complete range of hifi products designed in Britain and aimed specifically 'for European ears'.

This readiness to supply a divided market does not necessarily mean that the music business will leap at every opportunity to support musical innovation. Hopefully the examples above will have given some indication that music will change anyway. Developments in new technology cannot be predicted. Small teams of software designers like the German C-Lab company, whose program for the Atari computer, *Creator*, is in constant use in music studios and home studios worldwide, remain vulnerable to the constant tendency towards concentration in capital. As with the small American companies which developed the synthesiser technologies of the 1970s, they may well disappear during recession, or they may be taken over by the transnationals. But other small innovative companies can as easily emerge to replace them. And the power that their programs have unleashed has also helped the small, independent musical operator. The possibilities offered by technologies such as the aptly-named *Creator* sequencing program have already helped in the transformation of the music business through acid house and the remaking of dance music. This reinforces the view that the informal economy of computing, the world of the 'hacker', has already subverted any monolithic tendencies within any information-based industry, including the music business. The availability of cheap music-making technology, accompanied by the emergence and growth of small labels and telephone-based organizations distributing creative material on disk or through computer networks and modems signal ways in which musical innovation will remain alive and well even in the forthcoming era of globalized leisure industries. Music doesn't have to be what already happens. And it won't be. History isn't finished yet.

GLOSSARY

ANALOGUE A wave-pattern model of sound, used in some kinds of tape recording and in early SYNTHESIZERS. Analogue sounds tend to be 'dirtier' than their **DIGITAL** counterparts.

ARTIST The person or persons whose name appears on a record as the performer of the music. This could be a singer (Linda Ronstadt), a band or orchestra (Jefferson Airplane, the Vienna Philharmonic), or a **MIXER** or **PRODUCER** (Paul Hardcastle). The named artist is not necessarily the composer or songwriter.

CASSETTE A small box containing magnetic tape. We usually know it in the form of the Compact Cassette, introduced primarily as a dictation device in the late 1960s. Within a decade of its introduction, improvements in tape technology and reliability made the compact cassette bearable as a music recording device, to the annoyance of the record industry. Philips, the inventor of the format, has announced a **DIGITAL** version which will be compatible with existing tapes – unlike the other digital tape format, **DAT**.

CD Compact Disc. A small circular piece of plastic which carries a pattern of dots. When these are read by a laser, they appear as digital information, which can then be converted into sound, vision or any other form of communication. The **SOFTWARE** format of the 1980s, in its most primitive form as a source of music reproduction, the CD promises also to be the format of the 1990s and beyond. CD-E, or erasable CD, will become a recording format to replace tape in all its forms. CD-I, or interactive CD, will offer integrated text, sound and vision facilities;

electronic magazines and television programmes are obvious commercial possibilities, but CD-I's real importance may well be as the educational medium of the future, enabling students to learn and to measure their own progress. The dangers of this system, standardization and routinization of creativity, may outweigh its advantages in user-friendliness.

CRASH What a computer does when it stops operating correctly (very bad news). Usually, the screen image 'freezes' and anything in the computer's random memory is lost. This can be annoying after several hours' work in the studio, and extremely annoying if it happens during a stage performance. Morals: keep saving to disk; keep backup disks; or abandon computers altogether and learn to play the guitar.

DAT Digital Audio Tape. A recording format using small **CASSETTES**. The technology uses rotating heads like those on video recorders to pattern a magnetic tape with digital information.

DIGITAL Using numbers to model sound, rather than the wave patterns associated with **ANALOGUE** recording devices and synthesizers.

DRUM MACHINE a.k.a. 'beatbox'. One of the most important of all electronic musical instruments. The precise rhythms produced by drum machines controlled the way some popular music was made from the late 1970s (especially hip-hop), forcing human drummers to change their technique. The sound of some machines, notably the Roland TR808 and the Linn Drum, have become 'classic', and in the age of the

SAMPLER, these sounds have remained part of popular music in the 1990s. Recently devices like 'human touch' have allowed human drummers to gain some revenge, by enabling their playing to control drum machines.

ELECTROACOUSTIC MUSIC A form of music involving simultaneous live performance and pre-recorded sound on **SEQUENCER** or tape. Strictly speaking, a great many popular music gigs are 'electroacoustic'. But as you might guess from the length of the word, it is usually used only by the more pretentious college-trained musicians and composers.

ENGINEER One who is directly responsible for the transmission of sound into recorded or broadcast form. The engineer will make sure all the machinery in use is working, and correctly connected, and will monitor sound levels to check for possible overload or distortion.

GIG Any public performance of music. Musicians of all sorts call what they do in public 'gigs'; audiences for classical music often prefer the term 'concert'.

HARDWARE A device built to perform certain tasks. Often the task, or a few tasks, are fixed: a CD player won't play space invaders. Some hardware can be programmed to perform different things according to the **SOFTWARE** instructions. So a computer will play space invaders, or it will play your latest tune, or it will do your accounts, according to its program. But a CD player also needs software: the discs themselves.

MIDI The Musical Instrument Digital Interface. This is a detailed set of specifications which are part of the design of electronic musical instruments since about 1981. MIDI enables instruments to send data to one another. In the simplest MIDI set-up, one keyboard can control another. More complex connections enable computers to control all parts of the recording process, from the first drum

pattern to the final mix. MIDI when synchronized with **SMPTE** can also be used to synchronize music with video or film.

MIXER Either a) someone who balances the sound at a gig, sitting at a mixing desk usually in the middle of the auditorium; or b) someone who plays no part in the original recording processes of a track, who comes into the studio as a fresh pair of ears and reworks the material recorded. Mixers are often employed to give personal versions of tracks which have already been released; this is especially important with club dance music.

MODEM The connection between the computer and the telephone. Computers can communicate with each other via telephone lines, and can send and receive musical as well as any other form of data.

MUSIC A personal, social, historical, geographical, cultural, political and commercial entity which constructs and expresses emotional, physical and power relationships through the manipulation of sound.

PUBLISHER One who oversees the collection of royalty payments on the sale of recordings, or broadcast or live performance, of any material in his or her catalogue of published music. Today most publishers are only peripherally interested in the actual publication of sheet music.

PRODUCER Used to be somebody who acted as overseer when the **ARTIST** was recording. Today it can be the person responsible for the entire content of a track or album.

SAMPLER A musical instrument which **DIGITALLY** records and stores sound from any source. The stored sounds can be manipulated and played back from a keyboard or any other pitch controller. Almost all samplers are capable of use via **MIDI**.

SEQUENCER A device which stores a sequence of musical data (including pitch, volume information and so on) and can then replay it through **MIDI**. Most sequencers allow the stored data to be edited in detail.

SMPTE The Society of Motion Picture and Television Engineers specification. This is a 'time code', basically a set of electronic signals which is put on tape, and which when the tape is replayed can be 'read' by computers, thus controlling them. It enables videotape or film events to be slaved to each other, or via **MIDI** to musical performances, for editing.

SOFTWARE The set of instructions which program a computer and enable it to perform certain tasks, such as word processing. Also the discs, cassettes etc used in hi-fi equipment.

SYNTHESIZER A musical instrument which makes sound through the control of voltages passed through oscillators and filters (**ANALOGUE**) or through the manipulation of data on a microchip (**DIGITAL**).

FURTHER READING

This is a list of some interesting recent books. It is not an exhaustive list, but it covers all the areas discussed in this book – with the emphasis on popular music; cultural studies work on music still has something of an 'inverted snobbery' problem, although the selections followed by an asterisk (*) devote much of their time to classical music.

Iain Chambers, *Urban Rhythms – Pop Music and Popular Culture* (Macmillan, 1985)

Fredric Dannen, *The Hit Men* (Vantage, 1991)

Alan Durant, *Conditions of Music* (Macmillan, 1984)*

Evan Eisenberg, *The Recording Angel* (Picador, 1987)*

Simon Frith, *Music For Pleasure* (Polity, 1988)

Simon Frith and Howard Horne, *Art Into Pop* (Pluto, 1988)

Simon Frith and Andrew Goodwin, eds, *On Record* (Routledge, 1990)

Simon Garfield, *Expensive Habits – The Dark Side of the Music Business* (Faber, 1986)

Nelson George, *The Death of Rhythm'n'Blues* (Pantheon, 1988)

Charlotte Greig, *Will You Still Love Me Tomorrow? Girl Groups in Pop* (Virago, 1989)

Dick Hebdige, *Cut'n'Mix – Culture, Identity and Caribbean Music* (Comedia, 1987)

John Hind and Stephen Rosco, *Rebel Radio* (Pluto, 1985)

E. Ann Kaplan, *Rocking Around the Clock – Music Television, Postmodernism and Consumer Culture* (Routledge, 1987)

James Lull, ed., *Popular Music and Communication* (Sage, 1987)

Richard Middleton, *Studying Popular Music* (Open University Press, 1990)*

Christopher Norris, ed., *Music and the Politics of Culture* (Lawrence & Wishart, 1989)*

Steve Redhead, *The End of the Century Party. The Politics of Postmodern Pop* (Manchester University Press, 1990)

Sue Steward and Sheryl Garrett, *Signed, Sealed and Delivered. The Story of Women in Pop* (Pluto, 1985)

John Street, *Rebel Rock – the Politics of Popular Music* (Blackwell, 1987)

INDEX